A
MARITIME MISCELLANY

Volume 1

Whitby to Great Yarmouth

by

Dean Parkin

Tyndale + Panda Publishing

First Published 1989 by Tyndale + Panda Publishing Ltd.
117 High Street, Lowestoft, Suffolk

Typeset by Anglia Repro Services
133 South Quay, Great Yarmouth, Norfolk

Printed in England by Tyndale Press (Lowestoft) Ltd.
Wollaston Road, Lowestoft, Suffolk

ISBN 1 870094 11 5

Acknowledgements

So many people have helped with this book that it is quite impossible to name them all, but named or not I am grateful to them all. Firstly thanks are due to the staff of the many Libraries, Record Offices, Museums and Port Authorities who I have consulted: Boston Library (Toni Mather), Port of Boston, Sewerby Hall (Mr. Earnshaw), Goole Library, Great Yarmouth Library, Grimsby Central Library, South Humberside County Record Office, Hull Town Docks Museum, King's Lynn Library (Tony Lake), Lincoln Central Library, Wisbech Library (David Rayner), The Port of Wisbech (Capt. R. Kerr), Norwich Library and Great Yarmouth Library.

Also my thanks go to Peter Box, for his constant help and encouragement, Jack Mitchley, who has always taken the time to offer me some kind advice, Pam Stacey, Phillipa Underwood and Christine Johnson, who all helped with the text, and my travelling companions Lee Allington and Andrew King, with whom I embarked on a memorable camping expedition in the course of gathering information.

Two people must be specially mentioned. Arthur Credland, Curator of the Hull Town Docks Museum, who wrote the introduction and also provided so much useful information and helpful suggestions in addition to kindly encouragement. Were it not for his interest and help in the early stages the project may never have got off the ground. Likewise maritime expert Clifford Temple of Norwich, who gave me his time and assistance and indeed provided the impetus in the first place. His information about Great Yarmouth has been invaluable. To both these gentlemen I owe a great debt. Finally a word of thanks to my friend and publisher David Johnson, without whom anything is possible!

Dean Parkin
November 1989

Picture Credits

Boston Library: 25, 26, 86

Peter Box: 20, 87

East Yorkshire Borough Council: 18, 21, 22

Eastern Counties Newspapers: 66

Goole Library: 30, 32, 33

Grimsby Library: 37, 38, 74 (top), 92, 109, 110

Hull Town Docks Museum: 14, 16, 24, 26, 28, 34, 68, 69 (top), 72, 73, 74 (bottom), 75, 80, 82, 83, 84, 85, 88, 91, 101, 103, 104, 105, 106, 107, 108, 111

David Johnson: 12

King's Lynn Library: 48

Norwich Library: 59

Eric Reading: 52

C. R. Temple: 13, 54, 56, 58, 60, 64, 65, 67, 69 (bottom), 70, 71, 76, 77, 78, 79, 94

Wisbech Library: 44, 47

Contents

Introduction

by Arthur G. Credland

Curator, Hull Town Docks Museum

It is good to have a volume which does not regard the Humber as a barrier separating Yorkshire from the rest of Britain. The Humber was indeed much more a natural link between East Yorkshire and Lincolnshire and the counties further south rather than an obstacle; though close proximity might promote rivalry between Hull and Grimsby after the founding of the trawling industry in the middle of the nineteenth century. At the turn of the century the crew of the Spurn lifeboat, unique in being permanently resident on the station, were a mixture of Yorkshire coble fishermen and Sheringham crabbers. Coble fishermen could also be found making seasonal visits to Wells in Norfolk.

Owing to the vagaries of nature, the shift of wind and tide, and of changing economic forces, the various ports moved up and down the scale of importance and some ceased operations altogether. Hull originally played second fiddle to Hedon but the latter is now completely silted up and remains as a peaceful land-locked country town. It was the granting of a charter in 1299 by Edward I which made Hull the Kingstown and started her rise towards being a major port, a favour granted because the King needed its haven as a base for supplying food and munitions for his Scottish campaigns. The old harbour in the mouth of the River Hull was eventually to be superseded by an elaborate system of enclosed docks, the most recent built in 1969. Goole, on the other hand, was a totally artificial creation of the Aire and Calder Navigation Company and the town developed with the canal and dock system out of a sleepy little village.

The low-lying coast of Lincolnshire and East Anglia was particularly prone to inundation and a river haven or dock might easily be rendered useless by the deposition of silt. Boston was Britain's second port in the thirteenth century but the impact of the tidal surge had so undermined its economy that by the 1620s its inhabitants were emigrating in large numbers, some of them to establish the colonial settlements of New England, including the town's namesake in Massachusetts.

Fishing and whaling are the last great examples in modern times of the 'hunter-gathering' activities pursued on a more domestic scale by our prehistoric ancestors. There were short-lived whaling enterprises in King's Lynn and Yarmouth but it was Whitby and Hull which were to develop the trade to its greatest extent. At its peak in the 1820s the latter was sending over sixty vessels each season to the Arctic whale fishery in pursuit of the mighty whalebone whales. Modern factory whaling is immensely destructive of whale stocks and has become largely irrelevant in that there are substitutes and equivalents for all the products of trade. In the heyday of open-boat whaling in the Arctic however, this enterprise produced the oil essential for the nation's lamps and for use in a variety of industrial processes. Baleen (whalebone) not only provided ladies with their corsets and crinolines, but was a flexible, versatile material, employed in all those areas where we would now use plastic or spring steel.

Fishing, like whaling, has always seen the tendency to fish to the limit while the going is good with no thought for tomorrow. The inevitable result of this approach has been the destruction of stocks and the need to seek new fishing grounds ever further afield. At the same time, the result of overfishing has been the transformation of tons of fish into meal and manure instead of being eaten as a primary source of protein. Already in the 1880s the smacksmen were complaining about diminishing catches in the North Sea but the introduction of steam, combined with the fleeting system, masked the trend and resulted in ever greater over-exploitation of the available resources. The fleets stayed at sea for weeks at a time transferring their catches to a fast carrier boat which raced the fish to market each day while it was still fresh which made it an intensive, almost industrial, process.

The expansion of the railway network was important for the development of the modern fish trade, enabling the produce to be conveyed rapidly to all the major centres of population as quickly as possible. Fish, up until the immediate post-war period, was the major source of cheap protein for the mass market; the corner fish and chip shop became an institution. Nowadays fish is as expensive as meat and is eaten much less often, though is popular amongst the health conscious, demanding a low-fat diet. The railways were certainly good for the Hull fish trade and the North Eastern railway provided first-rate facilities for trawler owners and merchants. Similarly the Manchester, Sheffield and Lincoln Railway was largely instrumental in the launching of Grimsby, Hull's great rival on the south bank. For the merchant trade, railways, whilst providing easy movement of imports and exports, also provided the means by which trade could easily be switched from one port to another often with dire consequences.

New technology allowed expansion of the field of operations of the fishing industry. Steam-powered 'single-boaters' were fishing off Iceland by the end of the last century and exploring the Barents sea at the beginning of the twentieth century. Utilising one of the fish rooms as a temporary coal bunker enabled these vessels to make a voyage of some three weeks duration. By the time the vessel reached its destination, the hold was empty and could be scrubbed clean ready for receiving fish.

The huge fleets of drifters which followed the herring down the East coast caught huge quantities of the 'silver-darlings', reaching a peak in 1913 after which the great bonanza went into decline, though World Wars gave some respite for the recovery of fish populations in the North Sea. At the peak of the trade before the First World War some 8,000 Scots girls descended upon Great Yarmouth each season to gut and pack the herring. They were accompanied by perhaps another 2,000 men who worked in the curing houses. Stagnation of prices and rising costs were a feature of the inter-war period and after the 1939–45 hostilities the trade rapidly subsided into extinction and there was a complete ban on the herring fishery.

Concerns about overfishing led Iceland to gradually extend its limits until, in 1975, this was set at 200 miles from the shore. Their need to conserve natural resources for the sake of their own economic survival was to have a disastrous effect on British trawlermen for whom these northern waters were a prime source of cod and other white fish. The ports like Hull and Grimsby, particularly the former which had invested heavily in large capital-intensive stern trawlers, suddenly found there was nowhere for their deep-sea fleets to go as Scandinavia and Russia also imposed restrictions of access and a complicated system of quotas was worked out between members of the European community.

There is constant change owing to the dictates of population growth, the development of new technology, and the effects of the climate. If the 'greenhouse effect' we hear so much about results in a significant increase in sea level, then the east coast is particularly vulnerable to extensive flooding. Once familiar places will disappear under the waves, like Dunwich in Suffolk and so many of the Holderness villages which have been undermined as the sea brings down the low mud cliffs. Again, Spurn Point is not the fixed feature on the map many may imagine, but in a roughly two hundred year cycle has constantly been broken down and rebuilt again over a period of several thousand years.

Whatever happens to any particular settlement, the skills of the fishermen and merchant seamen, and all those who work in allied trades, will be needed to ensure that goods are moved across the sea and the fish is caught and processed for the nation's larder. The British are an island race, dependent on the sea for our livelihood — something that even the construction of the Channel tunnel cannot alter. There is a finite limit to what can be carried through one narrow trading link, and our contacts are not only with Europe, but America, Africa and Asia. The sea itself is a resource not only for fish but for oil and gas extracted from beneath its bed, and we must plan our exploitation better than we have done in the past. If we are greedy and careless the sea will be denuded of a potentially limitless supply of food and may be polluted so badly that it becomes little better than open an sewer. We all need to have a greater awareness of the sea and its value to us for our survival. Looking at the history of man's interaction with the elements in past ages we must learn not to make the same mistakes but husband the sea and all the riches it contains.

Part One

DOCKS and HARBOURS

Whitby

The tiny port of Whitby stands in isolation on the North Yorkshire coast, surrounded by the many cliffs of the area. The natural harbour, established in 1088, lies at the culmination of the valley and the Esk estuary, covering eighty acres of land which is often exposed to northerly winds, causing poor navigational conditions. Many of the locally famous coble boats can be found berthed in the three hundred foot quay around the town's bridge area, while the port also boasts a seven hundred foot fish quay. The Endeavour Wharf, also situated in the harbour, was built in 1964, with seven hundred feet of frontage space, while further along is a privately-owned wharf which can take ships up to a maximum size of two hundred feet.

In the early part of the fifteenth century a number of the town's vessels fished for cod off Iceland and the Faroe Islands. This practice continued well into the seventeenth century when, partly due to the Civil War, these prosperous journeys came to an abrupt end.

In 1820 it was recorded that Whitby had just nine local fishermen and relied on other merchants for the majority of its fish supply. Though Whitby supported a fishing fleet of its own, the main source of income at the time came from the Scottish fishing fleets, which were frequent visitors to the port.

The town rose to prominence at the beginning of the eighteenth century and at one point was even rated the sixth port in Britain, the result of the development of both the Newcastle coal trade from 1635, and the local whaling trade from 1753 to 1837. The town's whaling trade was led by Captain William Scoresby, who during a chequered career, caught two hundred and forty-nine whales in just ten voyages. Whaling slumped in the 1820s with Whitby's last whaler being withdrawn in 1837. With the demise of the whaling industry, Whitby turned to other sources of economic growth, such as importing and exporting goods and the upsurging herring industry. Whitby attracted visiting herring fleets to its harbour as well as trade from local fishermen at Runswick and Robin Hood's Bay, probably because the horse-drawn Whitby to Pickering railway, helped with distribution.

The earliest record of herring fishing at Whitby was in 1394 when the Abbots stored herring in their kitchen. In 1833 curing houses were built in the town to support the growing local fishing industry. We can therefore assume that herring fishing had been established for many years before the arrival of visitors — Cornish fishing fleets — in the late nineteenth century. Known broadly as the 'Penzancemen', the fleets came from Penzance, St. Ives, Newlyn and other Cornish ports. They were joined by fishermen from other fishing centres such as Great Yarmouth and Lowestoft and inevitably the Scottish fisher girls. As the nineteenth century drew to a close, the number of Cornish boats working out of Whitby diminished, apparently because a prominent herring merchant left Whitby and moved down the Yorkshire coast to Scarborough. Though a minor revival was experienced in the port after World War I, with an influx of herring drifters, this soon declined as most fishermen preferred to work from Yarmouth. However a small fleet continued to work out of Whitby and still does, fishing for cod, haddock, plaice, whiting and skate.

Looking down on the small port of Whitby in the late 1980s. Although herring fishing in the town has gone, the keel boats still catch cod, haddock, plaice, whiting and skate. Crab and lobster fishing is still pursued too.

The Autumn fishing season at Whitby saw large numbers of Scots fishing boats visiting the port. The photograph shows many of these boats berthed in the town's harbour.

W. J. Watkinson of Filey, known as 'Billy Butter' who commanded the first steam drifter to operate out of Scarborough, here seen on the bridge of the *Lord Kitchener*. Prominently displayed is the plate of C. D. Holmes, an engineer and boilermaker from Hull.

Scarborough

Scarborough sits proudly on the Yorkshire coast and today it is one of the most popular seaside resorts in Britain. However, the town was once a port of some notoriety with beginnings stretching back as far as 1225, when Henry III gave forty oak trees to the people of the town for the construction of a harbour. By then Scarborough was known to have both a fishing fleet and a prosperous trade in smuggling and both of these 'industries' were probably boosted when the harbour was completed. By 1251 a new harbour was needed, and this time it was decided to build it out of timber, iron and stone. However, by 1732 it became evident that it was too small for the larger ships of the day, so by order of George II Scarborough harbour was extended. Exports of provisions such as corn, butter, various meats and salt fish, and imports such as liquors, hemp, flax, coal, timber and iron were all regularly traded and encouraged the growth and development of the town. Recently commercial cargoes have again been seen in Scarborough's port, with chemicals, hardboard and wheat being some of the commodities passing through the port.

Another industry, which was once of some importance in the town, was shipbuilding, which was centred on Quay Street with the shipyards standing opposite the shore, though this feature of the town declined and by the 1870s was no more. The craft which were constructed here were mostly cobles, though some were of barque class too.

The East Pier was built in the mid-eighteenth century under the guidance of William Vincent, to whom a part of the harbour still stands as a fitting memorial, and of John Smeaton, a man who at the time was prominently linked with many aspects of marine life. It was the latter who advised the town on the problem of silting, though his ideas apparently did little to solve the problem permanently. The construction of the West Pier followed in 1822, replacing two inland piers, and today the daily fish auctions are held there.

In 1860, due to the astonishing development of Scarborough's fishing fleet, some alterations were made to the structure of the pier though even at the time, many believed this was inadequate, and the work met with much criticism. During the summer months the town's outer pier was let to local fishermen for dry-curing fish, which was a practice commonly used along the Yorkshire coast. They would then be piled up and left curing for just under two weeks. The pile was then turned over and left to dry once again and then packed up ready for merchants.

In the eighteenth century Scarborough, Whitby and Bridlington were the three harbour ports along the Yorkshire coast, with only Scarborough concentrating resources on fishing,

A busy scene in Scarborough harbour in the 1880s. A paddle tug-trawler can be seen in the foreground with a line of cobles behind.

A variety of sailing craft at Scarborough Harbour in the 1880s. Note the cobles tied up in the foreground and a ketch rigged fishing smack immediately to the left of the 'dolphin'. To the left of the smack at the quayside is a billyboy. These were single or twin masted with a clinker-built hull belonging to the same tradition of boat building as the keels and sloops. These craft operated out of the Humber mainly in the coasting trade but some also traded to the continent. Note the impressive bulk of the Grand Hotel rising in the background, built when Scarborough was one of the most fashionable watering places in Europe.

though the town was of far less importance to the Yorkshire fishing industry than neighbouring centres such as Staithes, Robin Hood's Bay and Flamborough. In 1813 the town was exporting so much of its catch that the local community began to suffer a shortage in their own fish supply. To prevent this happening, it was decided that all fish must be put on sale for two hours before being sent to various other markets. In 1831 two trawling smacks from the Cornwall area came to the town and caused quite a controversy with their new, successful system of fishing. Their trawling method met with some opposition, not least because some believed that these two 'foreigners' were stealing the local fishermen's catch. Despite pleas to the Scarborough Magistrates the two trawling smacks continued to work from the port, and it wasn't long before the situation came to a head when the town's fishermen formed a human wall on the beach and refused to allow the smacks to land with their catch. Discontent was fuelled the following year when more Cornish fishermen came to the town, bringing their families and intending to stay at Scarborough. Emotions ran high once more, this time ending with the stabbing of one of the visiting fishermen by a Scarborough man. After this occurrence Special Constables were hastily sworn in as a preventative measure, which apparently calmed down the situation. Trawling by visiting fleets became a regular trade in the town by the 1840s with the numbers increasing each year, though by 1855 Scarborough had begun to stake its own claim on a trawling fleet with the 'foreign' fleets slowly diminishing from that time. Surprisingly it was only Scarborough and Bridlington, from the ports of the Yorkshire coast, who showed any interest in trawling once it became a proven form of fishing. Over the next three decades the town continued to prosper through trawling, with its fleets even reverting to the boxing system alongside Hull and Grimsby. Steam was readily accepted at Scarborough, meeting with none of the resistance that surrounded the introduction of trawling. By the end of the nineteenth century the Scarborough steam fleet comprised approximately fifteen vessels.

The herring industry also brought much wealth to Scarborough during its many years as a flourishing concern, though of course this source of revenue was lost to the town after the industry's sad decline. Today the town has a modest fishing fleet, mainly catching white fish, with the addition of shell fish in the summer season.

Bridlington cobles in the town's harbour at the beginning of this century being used as pleasure craft. Coble fishermen often switched to this occupation during the summer months though would revert to fishing at the onset of winter.

Bridlington cobles, seen here circa 1930, were larger vessels than cobles from other parts of the Yorkshire coast. Note the rising board along the gunwale and the cuddy where the crew slept out at sea. These larger cobles also had a small boat on deck (known as a calf).

Bridlington

Bridlington lies just below the shoulder of Flamborough Head and was once known as the 'Bay of Safety'. This name could have originated in 1643 when a vessel carrying Queen Henrietta, wife of Charles II, ran aground at Bridlington and took shelter, while under fire from Parliamentarian ships. However, its nickname may seem rather ironic to the many fishermen who have found themselves trapped between the harbour and a notorious sandbank, the Smethwick Sands, which stretches from the area of Flamborough to Barmston. In the great gales of 1871 vessels became stranded upon the sands and many seamen perished as a result. But perhaps the saddest casualty in Bridlington Bay was not caused by the sands but by a German U-boat crew who torpedoed the *H.M.S. Falmouth* during the First World War.

The earliest reference to a harbour dates back to 1113 when it was bought by a local Priory. It remained the property of the Priory until the 'Dissolution of the Monasteries' in 1537, with materials from the ruins being used, unsuccessfully, to repair the wooden piers which had been continually damaged by storms. Before the establishment of a harbour at Bridlington, the town was a port of call for the exportation of Irish gold. The Romans are also believed to have made a settlement there, attracted by the shelter provided by the large bay.

In the eighteenth century, shipbuilding was carried out in the harbour, though on a small scale. Between 1820 to 1843 new stone piers were built costing £80,000 in total, then in 1866 they were extended under the guidance of engineer John Coode. The final design meant that the harbour entrance offered protection and refuge to distressed vessels from the cruel northerly winds. A battery of cannon was built into either side of the harbour but were never used, and suffered great neglect for many years until the Napoleonic Wars, when they were repaired and manned.

Though it is thought that Bridlington had a fishing fleet in the Middle Ages, it was not until the nineteenth century that any success in the industry was achieved. In the early 1800s there was still no sizeable fleet in the town and by 1817 only sixteen licensed cobles sailed from Bridlington, many of which only worked part-time. Its regular fish supply came from the fleets at Filey and Flamborough, with the town's own cobles often used to pilot merchant vessels. Bridlington was one of the first ports to accept trawling as a method of fishing. Many inshore fishermen from other ports were antagonistic towards the idea, and this helped Bridlington to become the most important fishing town along the Yorkshire coast for a time, forty-two Bridlington cobles having changed from lining to trawling by the 1870s. Another reason for the town's success at trawling was the soft sea bed in the Bridlington area, which was ideal for trawling.

Despite the size of its harbour, the town rejected steam power and never owned a first class steam vessel for fishing. By 1870 the town had experienced a fishing boom with the total number of cobles and mules rising to forty-nine. In 1875 Bridlington's fleet increased when it was joined by yawls from Filey, which had left there because of a lack of facilities.

Steam gradually replaced sail at the beginning of this century and at the same time, the Scottish fishing fleet became regular visisitors to the port. Herring, plaice, cod, crabs and lobsters were the main sources of income for the town. When the catch was landed at the town's quay, it was taken down to Hull in carts and loaded onto a train for distribution so that it was normally up for sale within twenty-four hours of being caught.

After the First World War the Scottish fleets visiting Bridlington for the annual herring season grew in numbers to such an extent that it was said that you could walk across the boats from the South Pier to the Crane Wharf Jetty, without wetting your feet! Though Bridlington later felt the effect of the dramatic slump in the fishing industry, it maintained its fleet through the decline and fishing is still a prominent industry today.

The 'Bay of Safety', Bridlington harbour around the beginning of the century. The paddle steamer which can be seen was called *The Frenchman* and was used for pleasure trips to Flamborough Head.

North Landing

North Landing, Flamborough around the beginning of the century. North Landing was a leading fishing centre along the Yorkshire coast in the early part of the nineteenth century and was relied on to supply many of the nearby towns with fish. In 1817 North Landing had forty-nine registered cobles but by 1869 the number had risen to one hundred and forty-nine. Its fishermen were slow to succumb to change and it wasn't until the 1870s that trawling was used in favour of lining with baited hooks.

The 1880s saw the beginnings of the obsoletion of North Landing's herring fleet due to falling prices. It was unable to offer the facilities necessary to handle first class fishing vessels and by the beginning of this century its fishermen had opted for inshore fishing instead.

Today Flamborough still has a small fleet of cobles which fish from its beach.

Note the building on the right of the photograph is the Lifeboat station.

North Landing, Flamborough, after the First World War. Note the difference between these cobles and the larger ones at Bridlington.

Fishermen with donkeys at North Landing in the 1950s.

Kingston upon Hull

It was during the Middle Ages that Hull established itself as a port. However, its poor facilities meant that vessels had to be berthed in the River Hull and rested on mud at low water. The port's west bank was continually overcrowded, with many ships needing to unload their goods on to smaller craft which in turn had to wait until a space was available at one of the staithes. Of the goods which passed through the port, the major exports were wood and grain while the main imports were timber, pitch and hemp, German hides and Swedish iron. In the sixteenth century Hull experienced a decline in trade after the export of raw wool ceased. This was eventually replaced by the manufactured cloth trade.

As the ships grew in size, repeated calls were made by shipowners for enlargement of the harbour. The request gained considerable weight when H.M. Customs added their voice to that of the shipowners. Finally, after much pressure, it was decided that an enclosed dock should be built to try to ease the problem. In 1778 the new dock, claimed to be the largest in England, was opened.

Nineteenth century Hull expanded rapidly with many improvements being made to the port. By 1802 an additional dock was commissioned due to over-crowding. Completed in 1809 and known as the Humber Dock, it did little to relieve the congestion in the old dock, and so in 1829 the Junction Dock (re-named the Prince's Dock in 1854), was opened, linking the two. The final addition to the town's network of docks during this period was the Railway Dock, which was built in 1846 and was connected to the Humber Dock.

A rail link, established in 1940 from Hull to Leeds, provided quick distribution of the catch and whole new markets opened across the country. Subsequently a line to London was added and later, in 1869, another to Doncaster, which gave Hull a direct link with the coalfields of Yorkshire, which proved useful in the impending age of maritime steam.

In 1880 construction began on the Alexandra Dock, which was built to handle the growing coal export industry. Opened in 1885, it was enlarged some time later, though it soon became apparent that more facilities would be needed as the volume of trade continued to increase. In 1914 another dock was opened by the North Eastern and Hull Docks Company. Named the King George V Dock at its official opening ceremony, which was performed by the King himself, it was again enlarged in 1969, with the newly built section being known as the Queen Elizabeth Dock.

Prior to the mid-nineteenth century, Hull surprisingly had a very small fishing fleet which catered solely for local fish consumption, although further trade was generated by visiting

Giraffes, which arrived in Hull's King George dock in August 1970 aboard the North Sea Ferry from Rotterdam en route to Chester Zoo.

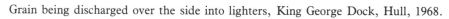

Grain being discharged over the side into lighters, King George Dock, Hull, 1968.

fishermen. When the Billingsgate Fish Market opened, however, many fleets moved closer to it to be able to sell their catch more easily, leaving in their wake a sizeable gap. Many smack owners from the south, who ambitiously fished further afield for greater catches, found Scarborough harbour too full and so decided to land their catches at Hull and Grimsby instead. They often moved their families to Hull during the fishing season, and many subsequently decided to stay there as Hull was now a prosperous city. This prosperity was due to the discovery of the 'Silver Pits' fishing grounds, off the coast of Hull, and the opening of the railway to Leeds, providing an excellent distribution service. The Silver Pits were to change the very history of Hull's fishing industry, but owe their discovery to mere chance. This occurred when a Brixham smack became detached from the rest of its fleet in heavy storms. Not having time to haul up its trawl, the nets were subsequently ruined but on examination of the tattered remains, many large soles were found entangled in them. It became apparent that this small craft had found a hitherto unknown source of fine fish which was to cause a surge of interest in Hull and the surrounding ports, and many more smack owners began to settle there. In 1854, thirty smacks were registered in Hull but in the space of just nine years, the number had increased to two hundred and seventy.

At this time Victoria Pier was used for landing catches, though later a corner of Humber Dock was set aside for this purpose. In 1869 completion of the Albert Dock (originally called the West Dock) finally gave Hull's thriving fishing industry a place which was their own, but it soon became apparent that the dock was too small. By 1880 the era of sail reached its peak with four hundred and twenty smacks at Hull and relief was provided when St Andrew's Dock, originally constructed for the coal trade, became available to the fishing industry in 1883, although it had to be extended in 1897. Around this period steam was introduced to fishing and the Hull fleet was one of the first to convert from sail to steam in the country. By the beginning of the twentieth century there were no large sailing vessels registered at Hull, although the Paull Shrimpers, small one man craft which worked with two trawls, operated under sail until the 1920's. The attraction of steam was that it allowed trawlers to make longer journeys to fish the rich grounds off the coasts of Norway and Iceland, and Hull was in convenient reach of the Yorkshire coal fields.

On the evening of the 21st October 1904 one of the most unlikely and tragic incidents in the annals of the Hull fishing fleet occurred, when the box fleet, fishing under lights, suddenly found itself under attack. Searchlights were beamed on them and a hail of shells from quick firing guns bombarded them for a period of nearly twenty minutes. The *Crane* was hit with two members of its crew, skipper George Smith and third-hand William Leggett, being killed outright while the other seven members of the crew all suffered injuries. Thankfully they were saved by another trawler, the *Gull* which had been among the several vessels also under fire with each suffering damage to varying degrees. The whole incident was the result of the hasty preparations made by the Imperial Russian navy during the Russo-Japanese war. The crews were badly trained and inexperienced and the morale of the whole command was affected by wild rumours about Japanese agents in Europe attempting to sabotage the Russian war effort. Afterwards Admiral Rozdestvenky claimed that he thought they were under attack by Japanese torpedo boats and responded accordingly, though the nearest Japanese forces were some 17,000 miles away! After an International Commission of Enquiry in Paris the Tsarist government paid heavy compensation to the trawler owners and the victims of the attack and their families. Henry Smirk, the *Gull's* engineer received the Albert medal for his

Victoria dock, opened in 1850, fell into disuse after the last war and has now been completely filled. This picture, taken circa 1920, shows the dock packed with vessels, including a heavily laden timber boat. Since the Middle Ages owing to its contact with Scandinavia and the Baltic, Hull had been a major importer of timber though this declined rapidly after the 1950s.

part in the rescue of the *Crane's* crew, while one of the *Crane's* crew, William Smith, received the Albert Medal for devotion to duty. On 27-28 May 1905, when the Russian and Japanese fleets eventually confronted one another in the straits of Tsu Shima, Admiral Rozdestvenky's great armada was annihilated. A statue of skipper George Smith was unveiled on 30th August 1906 as a memorial to the victims of, what has become known as, the 'Dogger Bank Incident' or the 'Russian Outrage'.

In the early 1900s Hull was regarded as the world's best deep-sea fishing centre. However with the onset of the First World War, the North Sea fishing grounds were closed and many of Hull's fleet joined the war campaign as minesweepers. After the war fishing was beset with problems, with overfishing and falling prices in the 1930s. By 1937, around two hundred and fifty trawlers sailed from the port — often the most modern type of vessel installed with the best equipment of the time. Many of these, with their crews, were the first to be requisitioned by the Admiralty at the outbreak of the Second World War and, despite many tragic losses, the fleet still remained strong on their return.

The years following the war saw the perfecting of the side-fishing trawler at Hull. However, fishing was declining as a whole and was on the verge of disaster when Iceland imposed restrictions on its fishing grounds. What resulted was the Cod Wars of 1958, 1972 and finally 1975 with the British fleets excluded from a 200 mile zone around Iceland. The effect on Hull was devastating. Hull's once great fishing industry became obsolete almost overnight, throwing hundreds of trawling-related families into turmoil. Many of the superior vessels were scrapped or sold to be converted for other uses, leaving Hull without a large scale fleet.

In 1975 it became apparent that St Andrew's Dock was inefficient and in urgent need of repair. The autumn months saw the gradual transfer of Hull's fleet to the Albert and William Wright Docks, with the old St. Andrew's Dock, home of Hull's fleets for almost one hundred years, becoming redundant. The new link road to the Humber Bridge made access difficult and a shopping and leisure development is now under construction in its place.

Queens dock, opened in 1778 was Hull's first enclosed dock. Access was from the river Humber up the river Hull and through a lock pit into the east end of the dock. Until this dock was opened the only place where vessels could berth and tie up was at the quay in the confines of the River Hull. Known as the 'Old Harbour', this congested waterway still had to be negotiated by vessels using the new dock. The Humber Dock, completed in 1809 was the first with direct access from the Humber and the completion of the Junction Dock (Princes Dock) in 1829 made the link with Queens Dock and completed the circuit.

The old Town Docks system was built in the age of sail. Many of the larger paddle steamers were too wide to enter the Humber Dock from the river, so had to moor in the basin immediately outside. Later in the nineteenth century the numbers and size of the screw steamers made the old Town Docks system even more congested and difficult for access.

The first dock to be built east of the River Hull, was the Victoria Dock in 1850, followed by the Alexandra dock in 1883, and finally the King George dock in 1914 just before the outbreak of war. It was decided to fill in the Queens Dock and here a steam lorry is seen at the beginning of this process in 1930. The area was later paved and grassed to create the present Queens Gardens.

Note the trawlers tied up in the background, newly fitted out.

Goole

The origins of a port at Goole only go back as far as the late seventeenth century when a consortium from the Leeds and Wakefield area began to develop the Aire and Calder rivers. Known as the "Undertakers of the Aire and Calder Navigation" they were authorised by an Act of Parliament in 1698 to make these rivers navigable and it was this same body which in 1774 were sanctioned to build the Selby Canal which linked the rivers Aire and Ouse.

The establishment of the Dutch River, which runs adjacent to what is today the South Dock and Barge Dock, also occurred in the seventeenth century when a Dutchman, Cornelius Vermuyden, unsuccessfully drained Hatfield Chase, an area to the west of the town. To make amends he cut a channel from the Yorkshire Ouse which was to become known as the Dutch River.

By the early nineteenth century merchants were complaining that the Selby Canal was insufficient and an outlet nearer to the sea was needed. The Aire and Calder Navigation finally bowed to the pressure and in 1820 were given permission to build docks and another canal, this time from Knottingly to Goole which were both opened on 20th July 1826. This was effectively the beginning of Goole as a port, boasting a fine harbour with two locks leading to the River Ouse, and also containing both the Ship and the Barge Dock. Trade began steadily with most of the profit being made by the canal tolls. In 1838 the Ouse Dock and Lock, (originally called the Steamship Dock and Lock) were added, the lock being fifty-eight feet wide specifically to cater for Paddle Steamers.

As the railway network grew around Northern England so did worries in Goole about the loss of trade the railways could cause the town's canals. In 1845 the inevitable happened when the Wakefield, Pontefract and Goole Railway Company were allowed by a Parliamentary Act to construct a railway to the Ouse at Goole. The Navigation Company had opposed the Act and had gained some clauses to their advantage. The new line was opened in 1848 and was operated, after an amalgamation, by the Lancashire and Yorkshire Railway Company. The Railway Dock was opened shortly afterwards and was connected to the Ship Dock.

In the 1850s the Lancashire and Yorkshire Railway tried to compete for some of the canal's coal trade. To counteract this W. H. Bartholomew, who in 1853 at the age of twenty-two became chief engineer of the Navigation Company, replacing his late father, introduced what proved to be a revolutionary idea to the port. Based upon the principle of railway transportation, Bartholomew's idea was to have a tug pulling a convoy of boats behind it. To load the boats into the awaiting big ships he had even invented a special hoist which lifted the boat and then tipped its contents down a chute. This system

A post war view of Goole docks from an overlooking Water Tower. After the war the port was nationalised and came under the control of the British Transport Commission in 1948. Though the docks were in a poor state of repair, they were renovated and modernised in the 1950s and by 1956 trade passing through Goole was in excess of 3,000,000 tons!

was used to take the coal from the Yorkshire mines to the seagoing vessels and helped the port of Goole to secure the coal trade.

There can be no argument over W. H. Bartholomew's importance to Goole. In addition to his post at the Navigation company, in 1880 he became general manager of the Goole Steam Shipping Company. Now, under his guidance, the Steam Company reached previously unparallelled success, with the first real achievement being the construction of Aldam Dock.

The 1880s was to see many improvements to the port, such as an extention to the Railway Dock and the introduction of navigational lighting aids and the widening and deepening of the River Ouse. The latter allowed Goole to handle the big 2,000 ton colliers, being no longer restricted to vessels of a quarter of that size. In 1891 the development continued with the construction of the New Extension Dock, later to be renamed the Stanhope Dock. The following years up to the First World War saw a time of prosperity for the port and apart from coal other goods handled during this successful period were dyewood, logwood, sugar and grain.

In 1904 Bartholomew left the Goole Steam Shipping Company after they were bought by the Lancashire and Yorkshire Railway, and turned his interests solely to the Aire and Calder Navigation company, where he was now both general manager and chief engineer. His last contribution to Goole was the construction of the town's biggest dock, West Dock, completed in 1911. By 1913 the port's total tonnage was 3,600,000 of which 2,775,000 was coal and it was fitting that W. H. Bartholomew, in the final years of his life, should see Goole's coal trade reach such proportions and when he died in 1919 he left behind him a port which he had helped to many glories. Sadly, in the years before his death, trade had begun to slump. The world Bartholomew had left behind was in a depression, nursing the ravages of war.

After the First World War, the port's trade had fallen eighty per cent with a ban now imposed on exporting coal. Matters were made worse in 1919 when strikes by the railwaymen and miners virtually crippled the port.

Trade had began to pick up in the early 1920s, with over 3,000,000 tons of goods handled at the port, though this was negated by the effect of the General Strike in 1926 causing the figure to drop to below 1,500,000 tons. In 1938 the Ocean Lock was built, reflecting the encouraging growth seen in the 1930s, but this impending success was robbed from the port again, with the renewal of hostilities in 1939.

After the war the port was nationalised and came under the control of the British Transport Commission in 1948. They faced the arduous task of regaining trade again and improving and maintaining the port's facilities which were in such poor condition. This period also saw the amalgamation of the Aire and Calder Navigation and the Lancashire and Yorkshire Railway. Soon repairs were being made to lock entrances and gates and new equipment was introduced such as new quay cranes and in the 1950s this era of change continued with a new fifty ton travelling crane being bought to replace the old hydraulic one while the Victoria Pier was rebuilt and Blacktoft was given a new jetty. Trade had returned and in 1956 was in excess of 3,000,000 tons again with coal still the staple trade.

In 1963, under new legislation, the port became part of the British Transport Docks

A tug tows some compartment boats through Barge Dock, Goole. Invented by W.H. Bartholomew in the early 1850s, within fifteen years Aire and Calder Navigation had over 1,000 compartment boats with a fleet of tugs, taking coal from the coalfields to Goole docks for shipment in the large seagoing vessels. A tug with a tow of compartment boats became known as a 'train' and though at first the tug pushed the boats, they soon reverted to conventional towing.

board. The new owners soon went about finding new markets like the Roll On-Roll Off ferries and container traffic with new facilities being built to provide for them. Improvements were carried out, which included overhauling the Ocean Lock gates, the building of two new quays in Ouse Dock and Barge Dock, the filling in of the harbour basin and new cranes brought the modernisation of out dated machinery.

In 1973, after poor trade figures in the previous years, there was a revival at the port. By 1975 the port's tonnage had risen to 1,800,000 tons, with the main commodities being coal, steel, timber, vehicles, grain, fuels, container traffic and general goods. In fact 700,000 tons of coal had been handled, the highest for almost fifty years!

In the 1980s the port passed into the control of Associated British Ports as successor to the Transport Docks Board. Over the years Goole has had to adapt and has survived the collapse of the coal industry, turning instead to new traffic and today specialises in terminal facilities, handling the storage of containers and other unit loads.

A coal hoist at Goole in the early part of the century. The first hoist in the town was introduced in the late 1860s and sited at Ouse Dock. Bartholomew invented a special type of hoist which lifted the loaded compartment boats out of the water and then tipped its contents down a chute.

Grimsby Docks. The tower was built in 1852 and is a two-thirds replica of the Renaissance tower overlooking the city square in Sienna. It originally provided a head of water for a hydraulic system which operated the lock gates and dockside machinery.

Grimsby

For Grimsby fishing was a way of life. Even the town's football team is nicknamed 'The Mariners'. Yet is was not until the nineteenth century that Grimsby began to gain recognition as an established fishing centre. Like Hull (in medieval times) Grimsby was mainly a landing port and had no sizeable or important fleet of its own. In the eighteenth and the early part of the nineteenth centuries the port continued to make a humble living out of fishing, though showed no sign of developing into a major centre. The origin of its growth must be partly credited to the Manchester, Sheffield and Lincolnshire Railway Company who brought a railway here in 1847. They were the predominant influence behind the construction of a new dock which was begun in 1849 with the foundation stone being laid by Prince Albert. Named The Royal Dock it boasted two locks and a hydraulic tower which powered the opening and shutting of the dock gates. In 1854 Queen Victoria officially opened the Royal Dock amidst spectacular celebrations.

Grimsby's growth as a port corresponded to the growth of the railways, which were making possible the quick and easy distribution of fish. This development was reflected in the town's population figures which trebled between 1801 and 1851. This increase was the result of the expanding fishing industry, which attracted vast numbers of people to the town. Prior to 1830 Grimsby did not have one resident fishing vessel but by the beginning of 1854 the number had risen to 105, and by the end of that year had astonishingly doubled to 211.

It was in 1848 that Grimsby's first two rail links were completed which were to generate the popular interest in the town as smack owners from all over the country moved their families to base themselves in Grimsby in order to participate in the town's fishing boom. To attract them to Grimsby they were offered such incentives as the free transportation of their fish.

In 1863 the Grimsby Ice Company was established for the purpose of importing natural ice from Norway to use in packing the fish. The company was to have a major effect on the town's fishing industry. By the 1880s they had begun to expand into different fields which included transporting fish to Billingsgate market. The same period saw the establishment of both the Great Grimsby Coal, Salt and Tanning Co. Ltd. in 1872 and the Grimsby Steam Fishing Company in 1881.

In the latter half of the ninteenth century box fleeting, where vessels fish in a group instead of independently, became widely used by Grimsby's fishing industry. One of the leading employers of this method was the Grimsby Ice Company who built up a fleet of some hundred vessels. However, the company's record was marred by disputes like those arising, in 1880 and 1885, when the Ice Company tried to goad the fishermen into fleeting all through the year.

Fleeting was a hazardous pursuit even under the best conditions, one of the main problems being the risk of collision between the many smacks manoeuvring around the carrier ship. So in 1880, when the Ice Company announced that fleeting was to be introduced in the winter months, around 700 smacksmen went on strike and the idea was withdrawn. However, the second time they attempted to introduce it, in 1885, the resistance was far weaker with only 60 smacks' crews refusing to set sail. This time the Ice Company had their way with the striking fishermen eventually returning to work. Fleeting was never popular with the fishermen and was discontinued after 1901.

The same year saw the 'Great Lock-out' at Grimsby when the fishermen objected to a new system of payment which was to be introduced. Previously skippers and mates were paid a percentage of the value of the catch but under the new scheme, known as 'poundage', the whole crew would be paid a share of the profits of a catch at so much in the pound. This would be on top of a regular wage. For the trawler owners the new scheme would reduce their outlay though it still offered the fishermen a bonus for a big catch. 'Poundage' was not greeted with much enthusiasm by the men as it would often leave them without enough money to pay for their vessels' expenses. So when the crews declined to sign the agreements contracting them to 'poundage', they were locked out and the whole trawler fleet was laid up.

Henry Smethurst, the Chairman of the Ice Company, lived up to his unscrupulous reputation, when he tried to man his trawlers with foreign crews. This only served to provoke more trouble and a tumultuous crowd of angry fishermen gathered outside his offices. Soon the mob developed into a riot which spread throughout the town leaving destruction in its wake. This at least highlighted the men's problem, for they were now desperate and poverty stricken after only a few months of the strike. The Board of Trade's arbitrator investigated the matter with his decision giving the fishermen a wage only a little better than the original offer. But by this time the fishermen's resolve had been shattered and the dispute, which lasted from July to October, ended with 'poundage' being introduced.

In 1882 the Grimsby Steam Fishing Company was responsible for introducing to the town their first two steam trawlers, the *Zodiac* and the *Aries*, costing around £3,500 each. By the beginning of the twentieth century there were 478 steam trawlers but only 34 sailing smacks remaining as many smack owners were already forced out of business, unable to compete with the faster and more efficent steam trawlers.

During the two wars Grimsby's trawling industry played its part in catering for England's rising demand for fish, simply because it was a cheap and nutritious food. However both white fishing and herring lost trade when exports from Britain to German and Russian markets were closed. In the years after the First World War around 7,000 men were earning their living from the Grimsby fishing industry with 21,000 in support industries.

The Post-war years have seen the decline of Grimsby, along with many other ports, as a landing centre. In the 1950s long-distance fishing expeditions to areas around the Scandinavian coasts provided Grimsby with just under half of the town's total catch so when in 1958 Iceland imposed a twelve-mile fishing limit round their coast a feeling

Smacks in Grimsby's first fish dock, taken in the early 1870's.

General view of Grimsby Dock showing the Fish Market and Steam Trawlers.

of resentment spread through the fishing fleets. And so began the first of three 'Cod Wars' (subsequently repeated in 1972 and 1975), with the British authorities conceding to Iceland's extended fishing limits each time.

The Cod Wars saw Iceland fight and attack British fisherman causing the fleets to fish in packs under Royal Navy protection. The fleets' warps were cut and even shells were fired as the Icelanders sought to defend their claimed area. Each extension of the limit had a crushing effect on Grimsby's fishing industry and in 1976 Britain accepted Iceland's two hundred mile fishing limit. The final blows were the total exclusion of British trawlers from the White Sea, Barents Sea, Faroe Islands and from the coasts of Norway, Greenland and Newfoundland between 1976-78, an area which had provided the Grimsby fleets with nearly three-quarters of their catch in 1974. Grimsby's deep sea fisheries had been destroyed.

Today Grimsby's fishing fleet is made up of pair-trawlers (two boats dragging one net) and Seiners (small vessels which get their name from the type of net they use). Fish is still brought to the town but now it is usually in container trucks imported from European ports. Many men still retain bitter memories of those 'Cod Wars' and the way the town's fishing industry was allowed to decline. Grimsby is now a large fish processing centre rather than a fishing and landing centre and any resurgance of the fleet would require widespread modernisation and re-development.

A view of Grimsby's Royal Dock. Behind the *Aquarius*, an early trawler with an open bridge aft of the funnel, can be seen the G.C.R. tug *Marple*. Opposite to the tug are ice barques while a collier brig can be found to the left of the photograph.

Boston

It was during the twelfth century that Boston began to grow and started to gain recognition as a seaport though there had been a port in existence in the town since before the Norman conquest. Among the town's earliest trades were herring fishing and salt-making, and later shipbuilding, though only the smaller vessels were built. Boston began to thrive, with both the export of wool and a weaving industry adding to the town's new-found prosperity. Wines from the continent were also a regular feature of trade. Lead mined in Derbyshire was also brought to the port, mainly for export to France, though later shipments were sent to other destinations, such as when lead was used in building an extension to the Tower of London.

In 1204 Boston was granted a town charter by King John, with the port then rising to a peak position of national prominence as the second most important port in the country after London. Merchants' taxes also increased accordingly, and apart from London's, Boston's charges were the highest in the country.

In 1236 a new era began, a fifty year period which was to see Boston's population devastated and the town's way of life completely changed, for this was the era of the tidal surge. These years saw Boston struggle through many hardships and it seems likely that it only survived due to a slump at the neighbouring inland port of Lincoln, which caused the wool trade to switch its resources to the town in 1369. However Boston was destined to see hard times again when just a hundred years later, the Witham estuary became silted up, and the port's trade began to wane. In the 14th century Boston was hit with another disaster when the Black Death killed many of those who had survived the return of severe flooding.

By the 1530s it seemed as if Boston's days as a port were effectively over, with its quays, yards and warehouses abandoned and left to fall into a state of disrepair. Many of the townspeople could take no more, as it seemed that Boston no longer had any future to offer them or their children or even their children's children. In the 1620s many sailed west to the new world of America in search of a better life. Once they arrived there they founded Boston, Massachusetts, thus establishing links between the two 'Bostons' situated on opposite sides of the Atlantic, which are still strong to this day.

The port of Boston lay almost dormant for over a hundred years, with King's Lynn taking most of its trade, until the latter half of the eighteenth century when both John Smeaton and, some time later, John Rennie were called in to suggest improvements to Boston's river facilities. Among the ideas in Smeaton's report of 1761 was one suggestion for the introduction of new drains and sluices, to help regulate the flow of the

Boston. The Dock.

A photograph of Boston Dock, taken in the early part of this century. Boston Dock was built in the early 1880s, covering an area of about 7 acres. In the Dock, cargo vessels berth at the North, West End and South Quays while tidal berths are available at the Riverside Quay on the North bank of the river. Within the area of the dock is a railway network, with approximately six miles of track connected with British Rail's lines via the swing bridge over the river.

water. This idea eventually lead to the construction of a Grand Sluice on the River Witham, upstream from Boston, in 1764. John Rennie's surveys of Boston's northern fens between 1799 and 1800 concluded that all Fenland drains should be deepened and given one way sluice flaps. Rennie's idea was carried out over the following fifteen years and proved to be relatively successful.

Many improvements were made in and around Boston's port during this period, including the re-building of the town's riverside quays. This resulted in new trade being attracted to the port, such as sailing ships with cargoes of timber from the Baltic, which became a regular sight in the harbour around the 1830s. Although new trade was coming to the port, Boston was also losing trade, for the town's harbour was continually silted and, in the winter, freezing waterways discouraged ship owners from the port. Indeed, the nature of Boston's waters were letting the town down again and what was considered to be the most dangerous of all haven entrances did nothing to help developing trade. There was even talk of bringing a railway to the town in 1836, in the hope that this would prove advantageous to Boston as a port, though it was not until the late 1840s that it was finally achieved.

During the 1830s there was the presence of steamships at Boston, carrying cargoes such as farm produce, sometimes from as far afield as the Holland fens. The railways however had the reverse effect to that hoped for, as the period spanning some thirty years from 1850 onwards saw Boston lose both its farm produce and coal trades, which were now transported by rail from the Midlands to London. The town was left to rely on timber imported from the Baltic.

After long and intensive arguments about what improvements should be made to the Haven were resolved, in 1879 the Corporation agreed with the Witham Drainage Commissioners and the Black Sluice Commissioners, to share the cost as well. The improvements were approved by an act of Parliament in 1880 and in 1882 started. The main feature of the scheme was the construction of a new dock with work beginning in June 1882.

The first vessel to use the new dock was a 241 foot screw steamship, the *Myrtle* from Sunderland, on 15th December 1884, amidst the cheers of an awaiting crowd. The dock basin was 834 feet long and covered an area of approximately 7 acres. New granaries and warehouses were built, as well as a railway connection between the Great Northern Railway goods yard and the dock owned railway tracks. During the same period a channel called the Witham Outfall Cut, running from Hobhole Sluice through Scalp Sand, was also constructed, and was opened to shipping on the 23rd April 1884.

These improvements began to have a welcome effect on Boston's expanding trade with most commodities such as timber, imported grain, and general goods, as well as its main export of coal, all showing an increase. New timber yards and saw-mills were also built to cope with demand. After the construction of the dock the port began to grow and attract new trade. In 1900 the total tonnage of goods passed through the port stood at 381,262 tons which by 1910 had almost doubled to 701,095 tons.

Trawling was also introduced to Boston in 1886 and continued there with a varying degree of success until the beginning of the Second World War. Few could have predicted the consequences for the town's fishing industry when in 1922 the collier *Lockwood* became

A photograph showing the collier *Lockwood*, which became stranded in the river at Boston in 1922. It subsequently became indirectly responsible for the collapse of Boston's fishing industry!

stranded in the Haven and laid across the River, blocking the way in and out of the port. Salvage experts failed to move the vessel so a Mr Parkes, boss of the Boston Deep Sea Fisheries Ltd, offered to do the job on condition that his expenses were refunded. The authorities accepted and Mr Parkes fulfilled his promise and moved the obtruding vessel. When it came to reimbursing Mr Parkes the authorities refused so the matter was taken to court. The judge ruled that the Corporation should pay Parkes £10,000, £2,000 short of his claim. Parkes, a councillor and a magistrate and reputed millionare, was indignant at the Corporation's failure to keep its word so he took his business interests across the country to Fleetwood, vowing never to set foot in Boston again. As Fleetwood and Parkes prospered, Boston's fishing industry never recovered causing Parkes to later comment that Boston's only chance of regaining fishing trade was for a new fishing company to be established to replace his own. Sadly this never happened.

The prosperity which was apparent in the final years of the nineteenth century continued into the beginning of the twentieth, with both imports and exports increasing. Coal hit its peak in 1923, and though subsequent years saw it still bringing in revenue, it was never again destined to reach the heights seen previously. Diminishing demand caused the inevitable slow death of the industry, until it finally ceased in Boston in 1972.

The biggest development of these times was the construction of the Riverside Quay just before the Second World War, which cost £60,000 to build. After the war trade remained stable with timber, fertilisers and fruit and vegetables among the most regular cargoes handled.

In 1913 the old town bridge, originally built in 1803 to John Rennie's design, was replaced with a £6,000 iron structure. In 1966 a swing bridge was built on the haven, this time costing in the region of £215,000, in a bid to reduce the strain put on the 1913 structure.

The second half of the 1960s saw intensive repair work and improvements being made to the Riverside Quay, included the erection of a transit shed and a grain silo. Though exports declined in 1968 subsequent years saw the figure rise once again, due to new ferry and container traffic. From 1970 to the mid 1980s the cargo handled at the port had tripled in fifteen years, reaching 1,262,556 tonnes in 1985. Today Boston claims to be one of the most successful small ports in Britain and offers large grain storage, Ro-Ro ramps, a container gantry and heavy-lift cranes. Timber, imported from the Baltic and White Sea ports, is still a staple trade, along with steel, paper, grain and animal feed. Indeed, Boston's level of trade now seems to belie its title as a 'small port'.

Three trading vessels, known as 'billyboys', line Wisbech quayside. Though most were built at or near the northern ports such as Hull and Goole a few were built at the smaller Wisbech shipyards.

A view of years gone by at Wisbech, when horses pulled barges ...

Wisbech

Prior to the mid-thirteenth century Wisbech was a highly productive port of some standing until this prosperity was upset by the silting up of the estuary. In 1236 Wisbech suffered the first of many tidal surges, with its second flooding in 1260 causing the town's once-flowing waters to become nothing more than a muddy creek. And so began a two hundred year period when Wisbech could no longer be classed as a port, thus indirectly helping to stimulate the growth of King's Lynn, which had previously been overshadowed as a shipping centre by Wisbech. For two centuries Wisbech was a ghost port, until 1480 when a seventeen mile cut, engineered by Bishop Morton, running from Peterborough to the town, allowed the Nene to flow around Wisbech's waterways. As the rivers returned, so did the quays and some of the trade, though the port had lost its independence as it was now administered by the King's Lynn Authorities. In 1570 Wisbech suffered devastating floods which affected all of the fen rivers, causing the Nene to be overcome with silt and also causing untold damage to many of the ports of the area.

The seventeenth century saw a steady influx of trade into the port of Wisbech, as the harbour once again became an active place. The prosperity generated by coal, salt and fish was to lead the town into a new era and over the next eighty years, the town regained its independence, breaking away from King's Lynn's control in 1647. It was around 1667 that the 'Coal Drop' was erected, which was used by river trade for loading coal onto ships from the railway. It was built by the Midland railway, who operated it too, and over the years it proved to be very dangerous, with men frequently being maimed or even killed, not to mention the loss of an occasional horse. The Coal Drop was eventually withdrawn in February 1904 when there was no longer enough trade to justify its existence. In the opening decades of the eighteenth century, wine, iron, coal, tar and hemp were among the many imports brought to the town, with seed and oats among its exports. Despite a scheme to try to channel the tide into a scouring course, by 1750 the way to Wisbech had again become blocked by silt so that no deep-draught vessels were able to reach the harbour. Instead they had to off-load their goods into lighters at Foul Anchor near Sutton Bridge.

In the latter half of the eighteenth century, the silting continued, making it possible by 1772 to ford the Nene in the vicinity of the new stone bridge which had been built in 1758. The area around Foul Anchor became shallow enough to allow a causeway to be built in 1826 running from Walpole Cross Keys to Sutton.

In 1772 Nathaniel Kinderley engineered and administered a cut from Wisbech to Foul Anchor, with the channel becoming known as Kinderley's Cut. About six miles in length, the channel offered a more direct route, straighter than the winding river which ran to the same destination. In the early years of the nineteenth century, Kinderley's Cut was restricted to use by vessels of less than forty tons, and in 1814 the first plans were submitted by John Rennie for an extension to the cut. However on the insistence of the Wisbech merchants, these plans were modified by Thomas Telford, with work finally starting on the project in 1827, with Wisbech financing £45,000 of the cost of the venture.

Further developments, helping to keep the Wash channel accessible and usable, included lighthouses built on both sides of the entrance to the Wash, two enlarged drainage channels at Crab's Hole, and the first Cross Keys Bridge built at Sutton Bridge.

The nineteenth century saw a rapid growth of trade in the port with the tonnage handled jumping from 29,242 in 1805, to over 70,000 tons some twenty years later. Warehouses and wharves were built, and flourishing new industries such as breweries, maltings, foundries and flour-mills were situated along the town's riverside. During this period thriving Wisbech proved to be equal in importance to its rival port of King's Lynn, with both towns going from strength to strength. Wisbech in fact had the upper hand in the first half of the century, though by the second half the position was reversed.

After the town hit its peak of prosperity in 1846, the port's trade began to slump, due mainly to the increased competition for trade brought by the railway network, even though the town's first railway had been introduced in 1847. A number of improvements were made to the port in a bid to win back some of the custom lost, though this proved unsuccessful and the heady days of the 1830s and 1840s were over.

On the 14th May 1881, after nearly forty years of proposals and argument, a dock was finally re-opened to trade in the town, with hopes that it would revive the town as a port and once more mount a strong challenge to King's Lynn's domination of the area. These hopes proved to be ill-fated as the day after its opening, the dock was closed because the entrance lock showed signs of leaking and its foundations were sinking. No attempt was ever made to rebuild the dock and it was left to fall into disrepair.

Wisbech has certainly never been a fishing port of any high acclaim with only two sea fishing boats registered at Wisbech in 1896. By 1911 the number had risen to twelve and the number was still small in the 1930's. By the start of the First World War, many locals began to turn to employment in farming. However, the port was still relatively busy with the timber trade emerging as an essential part of the harbour's economy, and continuing to be so up to the present time, with new quays built in the 1930s to provide facilities for the timber ships arriving from the Baltic. That decade saw the first cargoes of fruit enter the port from Rotterdam, as well as the construction of a new concrete bridge built in the town in 1931.

On 25th June 1946 the new East Quay was opened, at an estimated cost of £156,000. Funded by a consortium of the Wisbech Corporation, the Nene Catchment Board and a Ministry of Agriculture and Fisheries grant, the quay measures 2,000 feet long, and is built of sheet-pile and concrete. In 1967 the quay was extended by a further 1,200 feet. A feeling of optimism swept through the port in the 1960s as the tonnage handled increased each year, with timber and petroleum being the main commodities and grain the leading import.

The late 1970s saw an increase in the amount of imports and from 1977 to 1987 the figure never dropped below 30,000 tons, peaking in 1986 with 106,763 tons. In 1982 the port recorded a total of 253,248 tons, its best for some years, though since then has seen a gradual decline dropping to 108,532 tons in 1988. In that year the leading imports were timber (35,787 tons) and cement clinker (21,297 tons), while the main export was peas (6,247 tons). The port trades regularly in timber, grain, bricks, fertilisers (of all kinds), coal, clay, aluminium, steel, potatoes and animal feed, handling vessels up to 75 metres in length and of capacities up to around 1,500 tons. The port specialises in a rapid turn-round of ships and has four cranes which will hopefully be used to load and unload the vessels in the 1990s attracted to the town by competitive charges and good service.

Timber being loaded at Wisbech quayside in the early part of this century. Note the narrow plank the men had to cross when carrying the heavy loads and also the saddle on their shoulders to ease the weight of the wood and stop chafing. Timber has always been a staple import of Wisbech but in 1988 timber reached its highest peak for over twenty years, with 35,787 tons being imported, and is now the largest commodity handled at the port.

The opening of the Alexandra Dock by Princess Alexandra on 7th July 1869. Some time later the dock was connected to the Bentinck Dock, which was opened on the 18th October 1833.

A more recent and important addition to the Alexandra Dock was the Roll on–Roll off ferry berth in 1965, which has since proved invaluable to the port.

A timber gang at King's Lynn circa 1900. At that time timber was, and still is, a staple trade of the port.

King's Lynn

It was Henry VIII who renamed the town King's Lynn at the dissolution of the monasteries in 1536/39. Lynn's development as a port can be traced back far earlier than that, to the late tenth century, when the exportation of wool and the importation of goods such as wine began to boost Lynn's economy. By the advent of the twelfth century the town had proudly become the main port between the Humber and the Thames and subsequently in 1204, the town was created a free burgh with special privileges in the Great Charter ordered by King John. The following years saw Lynn rise to further prominence, becoming the fourth port in the country. Amongst the earliest exports from the town were corn, malt and ale, while among other significant exports were those of timber and wool, while the principal import during the medieval era was wine.

The port is situated on a tidal inlet and when the inadequate depth of water around the wharves during the reign of Henry III (1216-1272) was causing loss of revenue to the Crown, Henry made the townspeople a grant which enabled them to safely embank the swamps along the River Ouse, so that its waters could be channelled directly into Lynn's creek. Lynn was now a principal port for the wool trade, becoming a leading member of the Hanseatic League, and believed to be second only in importance to London. In 1570 new staithes and jetties were built which seemed to ensure the town's continuing good fortune. At this point however, King's Lynn suffered what must have been a major setback with the loss of its main import of wool due to a decline in demand, and as the Middle Ages drew to a close, Lynn's trade began to slacken despite the introduction of a new trade in the shape of British woven cloth. During the seventeenth century the town's economy began to recover when cargoes entering the port started to increase so that all possible navigational waters needed to be enlarged, due to the introduction of larger vessels. This century also saw the arrival of the prosperous and ruthless yet short-lived trade of whaling, (1753 to 1837), which had an immense impact on trade in the town. Two blubberhouses stood on the quay, built to produce the oil from the whales' carcases which was a valuable commodity at this particular period. They survived until the 1920s.

The Dutch wars of 1667 brought an influx of business to the Norfolk port due to the fighting in the North Sea off the East Anglian coast. Coal from the north-east, bound for London, had to be diverted through King's Lynn via the Rivers Cam and Len before eventually arriving in the capital.

In the 1760s the large fleets which were continually using the port were blamed for the worrying problem of silting. The dismayed authorities called in an engineer, John Smeaton, who was renowned for his design of the fourth Eddystone Lighthouse. He immediately set about the task of surveying the area. In his report he suggested, among other ideas, that the river should be completely cleared of projecting jetties and wharves, most of which belonged to the merchants who sited their premises by the riverside for their own convenience. Smeaton also suggested that tributary inlets should be filled up and replaced with drainage sluices set in a new river wall. By 1776 a selection of Smeaton's plans were put into operation, with the wharves being dismantled and a new river wall erected, but despite these efforts the silting continued and remains a problem to this day.

Though King's Lynn was still a leading port in the latter half of the eighteenth century, other ports in the country began to develop around this time and there was little growth at the port of King's Lynn for about the next one hundred and fifty years. The eighteenth century was felt to be a steady period for the port with corn still the main focus of established trade, although the importance of both coal (due to the industrial revolution) and the coasting trade to the port was growing.

It was not until the 1870s that new developments were made to the port. In the early years of that decade, a new iron girder bridge was built replacing the original bridge over the Ouse which had been opened on 28th June 1821 as part of the Eau Brink Scheme. The scheme is believed to have cost in the region of £500,000 and among the other developments to take place was the construction of roads on the causeways where once lay the old river bed. Prior to the construction of that bridge, crossing the Ouse was done by ferry, which must certainly have been a lengthy trip. The replacement bridge, completed in 1873, lasted until 1931 when a new concrete bowstring bridge was erected, which in turn was replaced in the 1970s, when a new bridge was built as part of the town's Southern Bypass Scheme.

In the 1850s it became apparent that new docks were needed to cope with the increased trade the port was generating. The foundation stone of the first dock was laid in March 1868, and in July 1869 the dock was opened by Princess Alexandra, after whom it was named. This dock was eventually linked to the Bentinck Dock which was opened on the 18th October 1883. The two docks were connected by a passage and gates which were crossed over by two electro-hydraulic swing bridges. Both bridges were further improved in the 1870s and still serve the town today. There were occasional setbacks too, with a newly built grain workhouse being destroyed by fire — and the coal trade suffering seriously with the advent of a new fuel, petrol.

The nineteenth century also saw the development of navigation and the River Ouse widened to a standard 300 feet in 1834. Three years later work began on the controversial Cut, which was to run through land to Hunstanton making a straighter deeper channel for the Ouse. The work was delegated to Samuel Morton Peto, a highly reputable contractor, who completed the three mile channel by 1843. The success of this much-maligned project eliminated the use of treacherous harbour approaches to King's Lynn. In 1848 the town was linked with a railway, running from the south of Lynn to the riverside.

In 1897 the King's Lynn Conservancy Board was established, bringing together the representatives of the various authorities in the port. In 1966 the Board became the Pilotage authority of the area.

The present century has seen the ageing Alexandra dock substantially repaired in 1933, and also the opening by Princess Margaret in 1947 of a nearby transit shed which cost

£30,000 to build. Steps were also taken to reconstruct the south quay in 1953–54 at a cost of £200,000.

In 1948 King's Lynn Docks were nationalised. Public ownership meant a subsequent series of improvements which helped King's Lynn to become one of the most modern and flourishing of the smaller British ports. By the close of the 1950s there were encouraging signs of new prosperity with the total amount of tonnage handled in 1958 amounting to 415,772 tonnes, the highest since 1913. In the 1960s both the town's docks were modernised.

First in 1960 the south side of the Bentinck Dock had 1000 feet of its quay rebuilt as well as improvements on the berthing for the coastal tanker trade. In 1965 it was the turn of the Alexandra Dock to be modernised with the erection of a Ro-Ro (Roll on – Roll off ferries) berth on its north side and the rebuilding of 800 feet of quay. Ro-Ro ferries proved to be a valuable asset to the town when they first arrived in 1967. This was the first such regular trade link to be established between Germany and England. Skoda cars from Germany have been the largest Ro-Ro import, with ferries still actively in service at King's Lynn today.

The 1970s saw a steady growth within the port and by the latter years of the decade the tonnage handled was repeatedly reaching record levels. In 1977, 1,060,463 tonnes of imports were handled, exceeding the previous best recorded in 1975 by almost 20,000 tonnes. This was probably due to the increase by almost 100,000 tonnes in the volume of grain handled during that year. The second half of the 1980s has seen King's Lynn go from strength to strength, with large exports of grain shipped to the Soviet bloc countries in vessels carrying some 3000 tonnes at a time. Commodities like soya meal and fertilisers as well as steel and timber, are all regularly handled at the port. In 1985, '86 and '87, record tonnages were recorded, though further growth in 1988 was hampered by the departure of Esso from the port, which had brought 170,000 tonnes of petroleum through King's Lynn in 1987.

Today, King's Lynn is one of the most important of the smaller English ports, ideally placed to capitalise on the ever-expanding European markets in the 1990s and beyond.

At Wells, prior to the mid-nineteenth century, ships used to have to transfer their cargoes because there was no accessible route for ships to the town's quayside. After the building of the Embankment in 1859 a new cut was made and vessels could at last load and unload their cargoes directly onto the quay.

Wells-next-the-Sea

Though most of the North Norfolk ports and harbours have suffered a decline, Wells-next-the-Sea is the only remaining port in this area which has maintained any commercial significance. At one time a number of livelihoods used to depend upon the local oyster fishery, though is of little significance to the port today. There were seven oyster beds in the King's Lynn area, all of which were overfished as a result of improved fishing techniques, and soon the fleet at Wells began to diminish. The town's last oyster smack was the *Little Polly*, owned by Charles E. Worthington, which was finally withdrawn in 1904. It seems likely that Wells had their own herring fleet too, which fished alongside the Scarborough cobles who annually 'migrated' to Wells for the herring season. In 1844 the town had a fleet of thirty-two fishing boats which had reduced to a couple of lining cobles within thirty years. By 1867 there were approximately four smacks trawling from Wells, catching soles, butts and thornbacks, though by 1875 there were none. However, fishing for sprats, cockles, mussels and sea trout continued and in the 1890s when whelking spread to the town from neighbouring Sheringham, which had become overcrowded, Wells's inshore fishing industry received a welcome boost.

During one period for every fish landed at Wells, as in other ports, the church took a tithe, known as 'Christe's dole' with the money being given to the poor and the suffering. Another tithe went to the port authority to help finance the upkeep and maintenance of the port. However, in 1591 the Wells fishermen complained to the local Justice of the Peace, Mr Nathaniel Bacon, that the parson was using 'Christe's dole' for his own means. On this occasion the complaint was overruled though such an occurrence was not unheard of at the other ports who participated in 'Christe's dole'. Eventually the custom lapsed at Wells when the tithe got so small that neither the church nor port authority bothered to collect their money.

Despite its size Wells was a major port in the days of sail and has always handled a varied range of commodities. Amongst the imports in 1854 were coal, timber, salt, rape and linseed while exports were mainly corn, barley, malt, oysters and the grain from the farms of North Norfolk. Today the harbour can handle ships up to 750 tons and has a maximum draft of ten feet with animal feed being its largest commodity. Although Wells has become a holiday resort, like the now defunct port of Blakeney, it has proudly remained a port which has even seen a revival in recent years, recording annual tonnages in excess of 100,000 tons.

Fishermen at Sheringham, seen hard at work mending their crab-pot nets on the promenade.

The North Norfolk Beaches

The decaying coast of North Norfolk and its exposed position has always discouraged the establishment of any harbours in the area. This has resulted in the boats of North Norfolk being small and lightweight, as the only means of berthing them was by hauling them up up the beach and resting them on the shore. One place where this occurred is Sheringham, once a considerable inshore fishing station, with crabs, lobsters, skate, cod and whiting amongst its catch. In the 19th century there were a number of curing houses in the town and over twenty large fishing vessels. At one time there was believed to have been about two hundred and fifty small fishing boats at Sheringham though by 1933 there were under eighty. By the late 1960s the town had fourteen boats but by then had lost any importance to inshore fishing it might have had.

Though Sheringham could never be classed as a trading port, Mr Henry Ramey Upcher, a respected citizen of the town, owned two schooners which frequently brought coal from Newcastle until the early 1900s. The vessels ran ashore at high water and were unloaded at low tide.

Another North Norfolk town without a harbour is Cromer. More famous for its lifeboat station, it does however provoke thoughts of its small crab fishery too. Cromer, whose bay was uninvitingly known as the 'Devil's Throat', had a constant struggle with the sea in trying to maintain a harbour and piers. One of the town's first piers was built around 1390 after Richard II allowed Cromer to have a percentage from all merchandise handled by the port over the next five years to raise funds for its construction. It was completed around 1390 though was eventually claimed by the sea. In 1580 Queen Elizabeth allowed the proceeds from the export of 200,000 quartern of wheat, barley and malt to be used for the rebuilding of the town's pier. Unfortunately by 1586 the sea had wrecked much of the rebuilding work and the pier once again lay in ruins. Cromer's history is littered with similar happenings such as in 1731 when the building of a new pier was undertaken only for the project to be scrapped due to the constant menace of the sea.

By 1566 Cromer had become fourth port in Norfolk behind Great Yarmouth, King's Lynn and Sheringham. During this time Cromer had forty-eight fishermen compared to Sheringham's sixty-nine and in the latter eighteenth century, despite the problems with the pier, the town's imports included coal, tiles and oil-cake, while the main export was corn. Cromer's coal trade proved an awkward occupation with vessels having to be beached at high water with the coal loaded onto carts at low-tide. Each of these carts would carry half a chaldron of coal as this was as much as the horses could pull up the surrounding steep roads. Cromer continued its trade in coal until the advent of the railway, the last cargo being in March 1887.

Cromer's fishing industry is largely based around lobsters and crabs though at one point boasted its own herring fleet which declined in the latter half of the nineteenth century. The overfishing of crabs after the introduction of the crab-pot in the early 1860's caused the Cromer's inshore fleet to drastically reduce in number. Today the town's small crab boat fleet, each boat traditionally painted red, white and blue, can be found on the beach near the tractors needed for launching them and is a living part of the history of the town.

Of the other towns in this area Blakeney's life as a port came to an end this century between the two wars when no attempt was made to prevent the harbour silting up. Blakeney was by then a thriving holiday resort and simply didn't need a port. However it was once an important medieval port, along with Cley and Holkham but gradually over the years the marshy channels which gave these towns their importance were drained and reclaimed and their harbours became defunct.

Cromer's small fleet of crab boats berthed on the beach. This type of boat has been in use at Sheringham and Cromer for both crabbing and whelking.

Norwich

By the beginning of the eleventh century Norwich was firmly established as an inland port enjoying close trading links with the continent. Developments included the construction of wharves on the River Wensum's west bank. It was this same river bank which was further improved, along with the Yare valleys, in the twelfth and thirteenth centuries, though it eventually became unusable by the larger ships once the river banks started to silt up again. This meant that exports and imports had to be taken to Yarmouth from whence they would be brought up the River Yare to Norwich by keel. Norwich lost all of its trade from the sea-going ships, and for the next five hundred years relied upon the river traffic with goods such as herrings, timber, steel, coal, cloth, salt, sugar and spices, and exports such as wool and foodstuffs.

From 1500 Norwich was hit by one disaster after another. The port was affected by a dramatic slump in demand for one of its leading exports, worsted cloth woven in Norfolk, believed to have been partly due to the continual attacks by the privateers on vessels which carried the wool. The period of misery continued, with the havoc wrought by the Black Death the root cause of the city's apparent ruin. Then fires caused tragic and disastrous consequences for the people of Norwich and her trade suffered as a result.

Despite these problems the population figure stood at around 16,000 by 1580. This difficult period proved to be only a temporary setback, with the city on the road to recovery by the 1600s. In the eighteenth century Norwich became a thriving port once more and went from strength to strength with the welcome return of local worsted cloth to the city's trade.

One of the main disadvantages for Norwich was that vessels bound for the port had to pass through Yarmouth, and when it became apparent in the early nineteenth century that Yarmouth was charging ships for entry to the Yare, plans were made for Norwich to have its own channel to the sea. With the co-operation and support of the flourishing port of Lowestoft, it was decided that a cut should be made from Reedham to the river Waveney near St Olaves bridge. The idea was that Norwich-bound vessels would enter Lowestoft harbour, pass through Oulton Broad and then through another new cut to Burgh St Peter. The last part of the journey would involve using the Reedham cut before finally reaching Norwich. Completed in 1831, the scheme did not prove a success as Lowestoft was still a young port and not enough traffic passed through its harbour to generate the necessary trade. Despite this failure, from 1835 Norwich was once again used as a port following a truce with Yarmouth. Sea-going ships once again sailed or were towed into the port of Norwich after a 500 year absence. However, the return of sea-going ships proved to be short-lived, as the railways took a large proportion of the trade which had previously been brought by sea and by 1900, only a small number of sea-going vessels used the port. Some Norwich exports did survive, such as shoes and

Sailing barge the *Will Everard* at Whitlingham Reach in the 1950s. It was one of a large fleet of sailing barges built and owned by the Everard family. She was one of four steel hulled vessels, all the others being of wood.

mohair yarn, and some imports as well, including American cotton, dyestuffs and cotton-seed, timber, wine and spirits.

The beginning of the twentieth century saw many schemes for the possible construction of ship canals around Norwich. All these ideas proved to be merely wishful thinking and came to nothing. After the First World War Norwich was once again classed as a port, with the diesel coastal trade and short sea vessels all bringing their cargoes up the River Yare into the port. The coal industry was booming in the 1920s with Norwich receiving a welcome increase in coal traffic as a result, while grain was also a major import of this period. A large increase in trade was felt the following decade, after the building of a power station and two grain silos and the general replacement of old coasters with newer, shallow draught vessels. By 1936-37, the gross tonnage of the port had risen to 257,000 tons, with scrap metal, grain and coal being the leading commodities. After the Second World War overall trade declined, with the major loss of the following decades being the coal trade. By the 1970s there was a steady flow of traffic in the Yare with timber and grain still the main commodities handled. Today more river traffic has been generated by the Broads yachts and cruisers which come to the city, alongside the numerous coasters which still unload at the port.

The *River Trent* of Hull and the *Formality* at Norwich quayside in the early 1950s. The port's main commodities around this period were coal, wood, and grain.

Steam drifters line Yarmouth fish wharf in the 1920's.

Bringing in the catch. The Scottish fishing fleet unloading at Great Yarmouth fish wharf in 1945. By then the fleet were entirely powered by steam.

Great Yarmouth

The town of Great Yarmouth is our last port of call, as we move round to the very edge of eastern England. Once it was the world's premier herring port, with drifters lining its crowded harbours, but with the decline of fishing, Great Yarmouth has turned to other marine-linked activities and is presently an important base for North Sea oil operations, another exhaustable industry.

The town was built on a sandbank and soon settlements of Saxons, then Danes and Vikings began to catch and sell the herring which came south to these waters each autumn. Thus the town was born, owing its very existence to the abundance of herring. The first settlers built their community around a church situated on the highest point of the bank whilst visiting fishermen, though at first occupying temporary accommodation, eventually built more permanent houses south of the bank which later became part of the Yarmouth 'Rows', an intricate network of houses and alley ways, some of which remain to this day.

From the twelfth to the sixteenth century Yarmouth continued to be a prosperous port though it began to lose some of its fishing trade to the Dutch fleets with their advanced techniques. Great Yarmouth was dependent upon herring fishing and it was not until the late 1700s that the town regained its lost catches when the Dutch could no longer fish the North Sea due to their involvement in the Napoleonic wars.

Great Yarmouth was granted its first bridge in 1417 which was eventually built in 1427 with a drawbridge added in 1553 partly for military security. This was replaced in 1572 by a bridge which lasted over two centuries until it was finally replaced in 1785 by a wooden structure, which had a chain and pulley system installed to operate it in 1810. In 1835 this was replaced with a temporary bridge costing £1,145 though it wasn't until 1853 that a permanent structure was erected, probably due to a lack of money. This was an iron bascule bridge which served the town until a new £200,000 bridge of similar design was built, opened by the Prince of Wales (later to be King Edward VIII) on 21st October 1930. The first bridges sited here separated the river boats and small fishing craft on one bank of the estuary from the big sea-going ships on the other side and each had their own quays which were also sited on opposite sides of the bridge. So in the mid-eighteenth century the town's fishing trade was centred around the South Denes and the beach area to the north of the Yare estuary while the coastal trade was conducted from south of the bridge.

The 1700s brought new sources of income to Yarmouth with the exporting of barley, wheat and rye to foreign ports in addition to the already established trade in flour and malt. With some ports in Norfolk showing signs of waning, Yarmouth began to challenge

King's Lynn for the title of East Anglia's most prosperous port. A flourishing trade in coal now made an important contribution to the town's economy with over 40,000 chaldrons (an old coal-measure holding 25 cwt.) imported annually from the Tyne. In the middle of this century the shingle bar around the harbour entrance made it only passable at high tide but the bar was continually dredged at low tide so that Yarmouth was not allowed to silt up in the same way neighbouring ports had done.

It is believed that Great Yarmouth once had a small whaling industry sited within the town, with blubber houses built on the South Quay. By the mid-eighteenth century seven whaling vessels were sailing from the town though by 1770 the English whaling trade ended as it was unable to compete with the successful Dutch whaling fleet. In the late 1780s a new whaling company was established in the town, no doubt motivated by the bounty system, offering forty shillings a ton, which was introduced by the government. At one point in the early 1800s the company owned twenty vessels but in 1820 it was closed, due to the loss of many of its ships and the ending of the bounty system. That decade also saw the zenith of the town's grain export trade, with some 480,000 quarters passing through the port.

It was around this time that Norwich merchants, whose trade had to pass through Yarmouth due to the unnavigable river conditions around Norwich, were unhappy about difficulties at the Haven's entrance and the heavy tolls having to be paid by vessels which wanted to pass through the narrow Yarmouth bridge. They decided to open up an alternative route by cutting a new channel, connecting the River Waveney to the River Yare further upstream so that their vessels would be able to use the port of Lowestoft instead of Yarmouth to reach Norwich. Completed in 1831 at an estimated cost of £87,000, this proved unsuccessful as many ships failed to make continued use of the cut preferring to avoid such a new, inexperienced and unknown port as Lowestoft. Most Norwich merchants continued to use Yarmouth's port, especially when the tolls were reduced to entice them back.

In the early nineteenth century fishing had become a consistently profitable enterprise in Yarmouth. However, as the fishing industry expanded, other marine linked trades began to decline, owing to the arrival of steam-power which facilitated long-distance transportation by water to the bigger ports, such as London. Lowestoft had taken a share of trade from the town too, until the Lowestoft to Norwich cut forced Yarmouth to reduce its tolls in order to lure back trade. This pleased the Norwich merchants so when in 1841 a scheme was proposed by George and Robert Stephenson to link Yarmouth with Norwich by rail, neither of the two places showed interest. Despite this a railway line was built between the two and opened on May 1st 1844.

The line, engineered by Samuel Morton Peto, provided a fast and reliable service, though transportation was still cheaper by water. In 1845 the Yarmouth–Norwich line was renamed the Norfolk Railway, before being taken over by the Eastern Counties, which in turn was absorbed by the Great Eastern Railway in 1862. In 1859 the town's second railway line was built to Haddiscoe, Beccles and Ipswich, again under the instruction of Peto.

Though being linked to the railway network with its faster distribution of perishable fish proved advantageous to the herring industry, some coastal traders suffered irreparably, with their number falling by half between 1845 and 1853, losing trade to the faster railways. However, these traders were not the only ones to be crippled by the railway as coal imports from the Tyne to Yarmouth also fell dramatically from 200,000 tons in 1845 to 20,000 tons by the end of the First World War.

In 1867 a new fishwharf was opened at a cost of £20,000, which proved to be money well-spent as it proved a valuable asset to both the local herring and mackerel fisheries. The new era which dawned in the mid-nineteenth century was caused by three principle factors: the herring industry, the building industry and the tourist industry.

At the end of each summer as the last holidaymakers were packing their bags, the town would prepare to play host to a different kind of visitor, arriving for the herring season from the north with the Scottish fishing fleets. As the Scots drifters began to collect together in the port, the Scots fisher-girls would begin to arrive in chattering hordes by train to make for the local boarding-houses where they would stay. It was their job to gut the herrings, and though this may not be considered a very glamorous activity, it was the amazing skill and speed at which they went about their task which gained the respect and admiration of so many. The phenomena of the herring fishery reached its peak in 1913 when an estimated 835 million herrings were caught by 1,163 vessels. The previous year had seen a record number of herrings exported from the 'pickling plots' on the South Denes, with 750,000 barrels, packed and salted, being exported compared to 126,304 in 1899-1900. However, after the First World War this degree of success was never repeated as the industry was plagued with problems, particularly overfishing.

Between the wars trade at Great Yarmouth did not reflect the national slump as its economy remained steady, with grain, coal and timber among the main goods to pass through the port at this time. After the Second World War in the 1950s Yarmouth embarked on a re-development programme with part of the East Quay rebuilt and repairs being made to the harbour entrance and the Haven bridge. The East Quay was a reminder of the demise of the fishing industry in this century, standing empty for many years. In the 1960s work was begun to restore the quay to be used as a mainland base for the drilling rigs.

By 1977 the volume of trade in the port stood at 1,015,000 tonnes and had risen 18% since 1966. The major imports were now fruit and vegetables, manufactured goods and refined petrol, while the major exports were foodstuffs and iron and steel. Foreign trade represented 65% of the port's total tonnage with destinations including the Netherlands, Scandinavia and West Germany.

In the 1980s the Port & Haven Commissioners spent £3.7 million on renovation work to the port, with work such as the complete renewing of steel piling at the North Pier being carried out at a cost of £362,000 as well as £130,000 being spent on repiling the South Pier.

In 1988 it was announced that the port would be given a further £620,000 facelift with this time the money being spent on the North and South Piers, Southtown Wharf and the East Quay. Perhaps the biggest and bravest venture was to be the Outer Harbour project which was launched amid a blaze of publicity in 1985. The cost of the scheme was set at £45 million and it was hoped it would create over four thousand full time jobs. It was heralded as a new era for the town, giving the harbour new facilities with terminals for containers, Roll-on Roll-off ferries, general cargo bulks and car imports. However, soon problems became apparent with the funding of the project and four years after its unveiling, the Outer Harbour Project is no nearer to becoming a reality.

The river at Yarmouth. The local tug *Richard Lee Barber* towing the Yarmouth built London barge *Greenhithe* up the river.

Note the Scottish drifters assembling for the autumn fishing season. The buildings in the background were destroyed by enemy action during World War Two.

Part Two

BOATS of the COAST

A wide range of boats shown at Yarmouth harbour bend in the early part of the century. Pictured are wooden paddle tugs, used for towing vessels in and out of the harbour, a steamship laden with timber, a Thames sailing barge and steam drifters and fishing luggers.

Shrimp boats from the 'Fisher fleet', returning from a day in the Wash, wait for the evening tide to lift them to their berths.

The fishing industry at King's Lynn operate from the Fisher fleet within the port estate. Around 40 vessels are Lynn registered and among their catch are shellfish, shrimps and white fish. Though there has been a fall in cockle and mussel landings at the port in the 1980s, there have been some promising signs for the future with exports to the European markets, while King's Lynn's whelks are becoming a delicacy in Japan!

Yarmouth shrimpers were small clinker-built sloops, around twenty feet long with a beam of eight and a half feet. In the latter part of the nineteenth century there were about sixty-five of these craft in and around Great Yarmouth, fishing approximately two miles off shore. As they were too small to allow room for a boiler, their catch had to be taken ashore and cooked in the fishermen's own homes with many sold direct to the public from the front room.

Shrimps have been caught in the Humber for several centuries using a beam trawl. The boats, mostly from Paull near Hull, when under sail alone used to tow two trawls side by side, one astern of the other. They worked in shallow water, never deeper than 8 fathoms. The gear would be down for a couple of hours, then one net would be hauled up at a time, and the shrimps, sorted by sieve or riddle, would be boiled in a copper on board. This is the shrimper *Venture*, one of the last, from a photograph taken in the 1950s.

The north-east coble. This vessel was always clinker built (that is with planks overlapping) forming a hull of exceptional strength and particularly shapely form. The ribs were inserted when the planking up was complete.

Square stern cobles were designed for beaching which was done stern first, employing the twin keels or drafts as runners. Pointed stern cobles like the large half-decked Filey and Scarborough 'mule', were moored afloat. The 'mule' was so called because she had a coble bow and a pointed stern like a keel boat.

The pointed stern coble, here seen at Filey.

A Great Yarmouth steam drifter leaving the town's harbour for the North Sea fishing grounds, circa 1924. Originally the vessel used for herring fishing was of similar design to other small trading craft of the fifteenth century. Known as 'busses' they were bluff in the bow (having a broad forward end) and had one heavy mast amidships with a square sail. Soon both foremast and mizzen were introduced and later a plain spar known as a 'vargard' was installed enabling both bowline and bowsprit to be discarded. This led to the use of a lugsail in herring boats, which in turn led to the demise of the buss, as the lugsail rig proved so popular that by 1850 herring luggers were being introduced.

Even the lugger itself was developing and between 1840 and 1870, a two-masted rig was added, which in turn was replaced with a dandy rig (a single masted rig with a small mast known as a 'jigger' towards the right of the stern). By the beginning of this century, steam began to dominate the industry. The era of sail was at an end and amazingly by 1913 1,163 steam drifters were fishing out of Yarmouth alone! Drifters are so called because they use drift nets which were and still are the principal method of catching herring. The nets are suspended from a line of floats and when the herring shoals begin to swim to the water's surface at night, they are caught in the nets. The meshes allow just the herrings' heads through but there is no way out for the fish as they are stopped by their gills.

Scots steam fishing drifters queueing outside Yarmouth harbour, to bring their catches of 'silver darlings' to the fish wharf.

On October 21st 1957, Trafalgar Day, the local and Scottish drifters took part in the first, and last, review of the herring fleet at Yarmouth. Admiral Sir Fredrick Parham, the leader of the Royal Navy's Protection and Minesweeping Squadron, saluted from the deck of the *H.M.S. Wave* to each of the 170 vessels in the town's herring fleet as they made their way to the fishing grounds. The *H.M.S. Wave* was anchored off the Britannia Pier along with other naval vessels and was passed by a seven mile line of drifters decorated with flags and bunting.

Afterwards, at a banquet, held at Yarmouth's South Quay, the chief guest, Mr. Derek Heathcote Amory, the Minister of Agriculture, Fisheries and Food said that, '.... although the herring fishery was going through a most difficult time, it had seen dark days on other occasions, and light would surely come again this time.'

A rare photograph of a Hull registered fishing smack. She is an example of the fully developed type produced in the late nineteenth century. Often more than eighty feet long, they were ketch-rigged and were at the optimum size for a fishing vessel relying solely on wind power. They towed a beam trawl which can be seen lashed to the port side of the hull.

Converted paddle-tugs were the first steam-powered vessels to meet with any success in the trawling industry. It is believed that Mr William Purdy, owner of a North Shields paddle-tug, the *Messenger*, was the first to convert his tug into a trawling vessel with any success, though it had been known before the 1860s for smacks to shoot their nets whilst being towed by a paddle-tug into or out of harbour. Though the ensuing catch was always inconsistent, this failed to convince Mr Purdy who went ahead with conversion regardless. This was soon proved to be a commendable decision with the success of the *Messenger* persuading others to convert their own tugs at a cost of £2000 to £2500.

The photograph shows the *Flying Squall* from Scarborough, one such converted paddle-tug, which followed Mr Purdy's lead. Initially these converted tugs were very successful though the costs proved prohibitive. The future lay in purpose-built trawlers though the heavy capital investment meant that the days of the owner-skipper were over.

The early steam trawler, *Albatross* (GY 279). Built by Cochrane and Cooper of Beverley in 1897, she was 100 feet long and weighed around 158 tons. Steam powered trawlers had the advantage over smacks of being able to fish in any conditions, not relying on the wind.

At the outbreak of both World Wars much of the trawling fleet was requisitioned by the navy for convoy protection and minesweeping duties. The Beverley Shipyard, near Hull, was commissioned to build a series of specially designed armed trawlers variously equipped with Oerlikons, Lewis guns and depth charges, and one of these military class vessels can be seen in the photograph. Many trawlermen passed through the famous Sparrows Nest at Lowestoft headquarters of the Royal Naval Patrol Service and they carried out the vital jobs of sweeping the shipping lanes of mines, anti-submarine patrols and the protection of convoys of merchant ships conveying much needed supplies. After the First World War the trawlers which were purpose built for fighting during the hostilities were sold and converted for fishing. Though some went on to be commandeered in the next World War, more armed trawlers were built, with sixty per cent of all wartime vessels being constructed at the Beverley, Selby and Goole yards.

The snibbie *Norborg H35*, a motor seine netter wooden-built in 1957 by Herd and MacKenzie of Buckie for the St. Andrews Fishing Co. Carrying a crew of four, she was driven by an 8 cylinder Gardiner diesel engine and was nearly sixty feet long. Snibbies arrived on the Humber from Denmark in the 1920s and though few are seen in Hull nowadays, a considerable fleet still operates in Grimsby.

The Danish seine is used for catching bottom fish like the trawl but is not towed. Instead a warp is taken out from a buoy followed by the net and a second warp with the boat circling round. Fish are persuaded towards the centre of the net by long 'wings' at the mouth of the net and the vibration of the warps.

Photograph showing the grandiose barquentine *Estonia*, known as the 'murder ship', owing to a stabbing incident which took place on board.

The barque *Shakespeare*, seen here during the filming of Boyd Cable's *Rolling Road* in 1926, in which the vessel was featured and renamed the *Gleam* for its rôle in the film.

Originally square riggers had single sails with a main driving sail laying square to the main mast though later developments saw the additional masts being added. Normally a square rigger had five or six square sails on each mast with a number of fore and aft sails as well. For this reason most crews included a sailmaker to maintain and repair the sails.

Barques and barquentines, now obsolete trading vessels, had square rigs, barques having three or more square rigged masts, but having the fore and aft rig on the mizzen, while a barquentine had only the foremast square rigged.

A Sail Training Association's schooner, the *Malcolm Miller*, rounds the Great Yarmouth harbour bend under sail on her way to the Tall Ships Race on Wednesday 29th July 1981. Largely used for the coasting trade, a schooner was fore and aft rigged, (a sailing vessel carrying no square sails), with two or more masts. The attraction was that they required a smaller crew than similar vessels of the same size.

One idea about the origins of the name schooner is that when one of the first of these vessels was launched, in 1713 at Gloucester, Massachusetts, a spectator shouted, 'There she scoons!', ('scoon' was slang, meaning to skim across the water), and the name stuck.

The Norfolk Wherry, *Albion*, crossing Breydon water at Great Yarmouth. The Norfolk Wherry's origins date to the eighteenth century when they began to carry passengers and deliver cargoes, such as barley, bricks, malt, stacks of reed for thatching and fodder for dray horses, around the Broadland waterways, as well as more valuable items whose delivery was always considered safer by wherry rather than by the Norfolk keels, which they eventually succeeded. Wherries had a single mast, which was normally free from its footing, allowing it to be pivoted downwards when passing beneath low bridges. The importance of the vessel's sail, which was painted black with a mixture of coal, tar, herring oil and lamp black, could not be under-estimated as most wherrymen believed that a good sail was more important than a good wherry. Though the largest ever launched was claimed to be the *Wonder*, which could carry up to 84 tons of coal, an average wherry was about 58 feet long and had a beam of 15 feet. It was this long beam, along with the shallow draught and black sail, that made a wherry instantly recognisable.

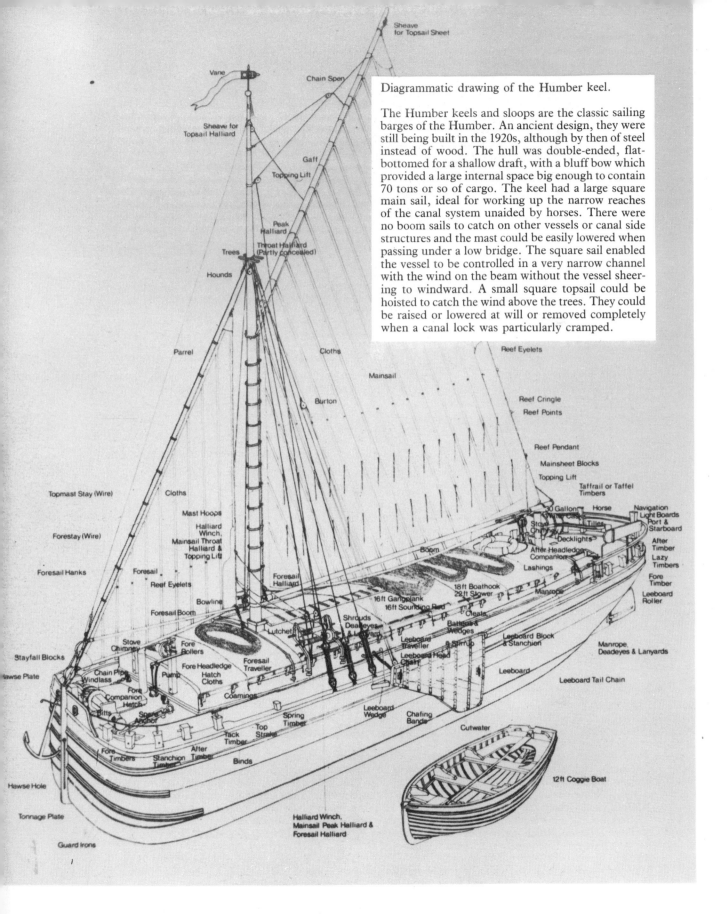

Diagrammatic drawing of the Humber keel.

The Humber keels and sloops are the classic sailing barges of the Humber. An ancient design, they were still being built in the 1920s, although by then of steel instead of wood. The hull was double-ended, flat-bottomed for a shallow draft, with a bluff bow which provided a large internal space big enough to contain 70 tons or so of cargo. The keel had a large square main sail, ideal for working up the narrow reaches of the canal system unaided by horses. There were no boom sails to catch on other vessels or canal side structures and the mast could be easily lowered when passing under a low bridge. The square sail enabled the vessel to be controlled in a very narrow channel with the wind on the beam without the vessel sheering to windward. A small square topsail could be hoisted to catch the wind above the trees. They could be raised or lowered at will or removed completely when a canal lock was particularly cramped.

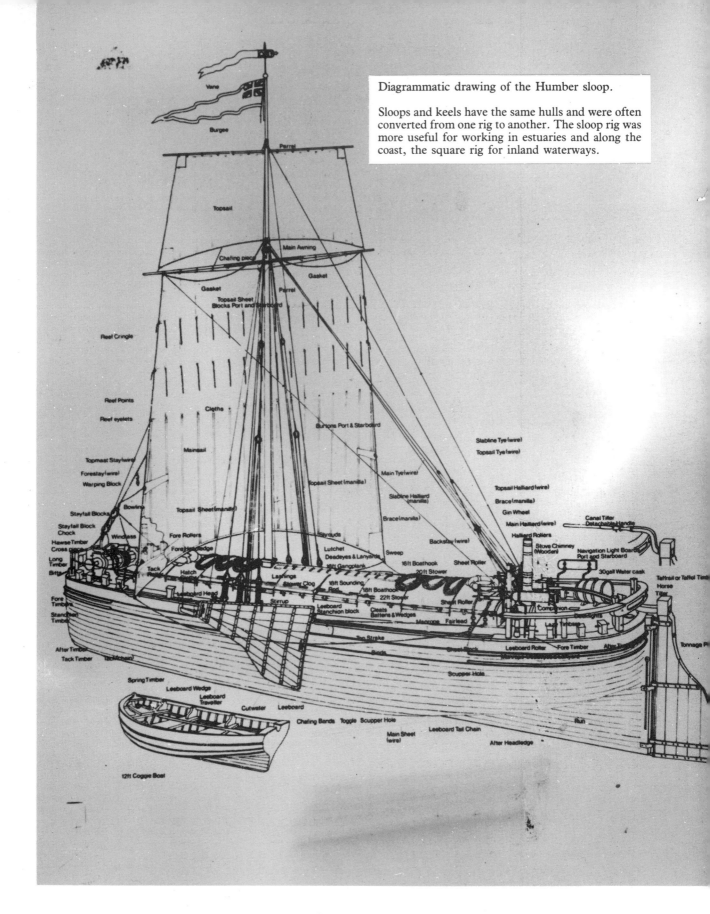

Diagrammatic drawing of the Humber sloop.

Sloops and keels have the same hulls and were often converted from one rig to another. The sloop rig was more useful for working in estuaries and along the coast, the square rig for inland waterways.

81

The Humber keel *Ada*, painted by Reuben Chappell of Goole. It was owned by John Gardiner and skippered by his brother William.

Trent ketch *Brothers*, a keel with the addition of a small mizen. This is a typical 'ship portrait' by Reuben Chappell (1870-1940) of Goole who regularly painted commissions for keel skippers and owners. This painting was for John Gardiner, the vessel's owner.

Montebell of the Wilson Line was built in 1890 by Richardson, Duck and Co. of Stockton. This 1,634 ton trader was sold to Spain in 1910. The firm was founded by Thomas Wilson who was born in 1792. After leaving the counting house of a local merchant and shipowner, he set up on his own, swiftly changing his fleet from sail to steam and absorbing rivals such as Brownslow, Marsden in 1878 while his sons Arthur and Charles acquired the entire fleet of Bailey and Leetham in 1903. This gave the company access to Portugal and West Africa and by this time Thomas Wilson and Sons owned nearly one hundred vessels operating to Europe and the Baltic, America and India.

The Wilson family had seen a remarkable rise in their fortunes. Thomas's father, David, was a humble waterman, while Thomas's sons had joined the ranks of the upper classes. Charles had become Lord Nuburnholme and Arthur, a friend of the Prince of Wales, had cut a dash on the social scene and was a master of the Holderness Hunt. Both were M.P.'s — Arthur a Conservative and Charles a Liberal.

When the *Lloydsman* was launched by Robb Caledon of Leith in 1971, she was Britain's most powerful ocean-going salvage tug. Her owners United Towing were formed in 1921 from an amalgamation of several small local companies and they still remain one of the countries major towing and salvage companies.

The *Lloydsman* became famous throughout the country for her work as one of the mother ships during the Cod War of 1975 protecting the Hull fishing fleet from the unwelcome attentions of the Icelandic gunboats. She was sold in 1979 to Singapore and was replaced by the even more massive *Salvageman*.

The m.v. *Melrose Abbey* was built along with the *Bolton Abbey* in 1958–59 by Brooke Marine of Lowestoft for service in the cargo-passenger trade between Hull and Rotterdam. At 2,740 gross tons and 302 feet long, the vessel could achieve a speed of 15½ knots from their 1,806 bhp Ruston and Hornsby diesel engines.

Part of the Associated Humber Lines fleet used the funnel colours of the old LMS Railway Co, buff with a black top separated by a broad red band. The initials were placed on the red band in large raised letters painted black.

AHL were formed in 1935 when the Hull and Netherland Steamship Co., the Wilson and NER Shipping Co. and the Grimsby and Hamburg service of the LNER were brought together under one management. Following nationalisation in 1948 it was jointly owned by the British Transport Commission and the Ellerman Wilson Line.

The paddle steamer, *Privateer*, was a popular vessel in and around Boston. Her career as a pleasure boat began around 1886 and she was operated up and down the river as far as Cut End buoy, a matter of about six miles.

The *Privateer* had many uses and in 1913 it helped pull down the old town bridge which was originally built in 1803.

Shortly before the First World War, the Board of Trade inspected the boat and considered her to be inadequately equipped with lifeboats, only having two, for the fifty passengers she was allowed to take. The tightening of safety procedures was a result of the then recent *Titanic* disaster and spelt the end of the *Privateer's* pleasure boat days, as to buy any more lifeboats would have been too expensive while a reduction in the number of passengers would have proved uneconomical.

The *Regal Lady* photographed at Norwich in August 1983. Built by Fellows & Co. at Great Yarmouth for the Yarmouth & Gorleston Steamboat Co. in 1930 as the *Oulton Belle*, she was widely used on excursion work from Great Yarmouth up to the Second World War. She was in naval use on the Clyde and is reputed to have been at Dunkirk. Considerably rebuilt after the war, in 1954 she was sold to Scarborough Cruises Ltd. and renamed *Regal Lady*, she ran various cruises along the Yorkshire coast until 1970 when she was sold to J. N. Blake and based in Norwich running trips along the Wensum.

After being laid up at St. Olaves she was sold in late 1986 to Machin & Garside and returned to Scarborough in January 1987 where a new wheelhouse was fitted for her new coastal services.

The interior of a Grimsby net factory c.1900. The women sat at benches braiding the nets which are hung over a rail in front of them. This was a labour intensive operation and no machinery is in evidence.

In Hull it was usual for the women to make sections of net at home in their terraced houses on the Hessle Road, the heart of the fishing community. A brass rail was fixed to the outside wall for working outside when weather permitted, though otherwise the braiding was done indoors. The various small pieces supplied by each worker were then taken to the fish dock for assembly into the finished trawl net.

Part Three

FISHING

Fish has always been a staple part of the British diet but its development was hampered by the problems of distribution due to poor roads across Britain. The introduction of the railway network in the nineteenth century met with the public's demand for cheap nourishment and caused the industry to enter a prosperous period which was to see the trade touch heights which have never been reached since. Here we examine the various types of fishing, some of which are no longer pursued, which have all in one way or another seen both growth and decline.

Most fishermen used to begin their life at sea inshore fishing. As youngsters they would join the older fishermen catching shellfish such as crabs, lobsters, cockles and mussels.

The advent of the railways gave these small fisheries a wider market, with new methods having to be introduced to cope with the demand. The equipment used for crabbing was a metal hoop with its inner area covered by a net, to which bait was attached. The hoop would then be lowered onto the seabed and brought up again at regular intervals to see if any crabs had been lured onto the baited net. Unfortunately fishermen could only set a small number of traps owing to the amount of attention they needed so when demand increased, 'trunking' could no longer keep pace. This resulted in the introduction of the creel or pot, which has two funnel shaped entrances through which the crab or lobster is enticed by the bait and once in the creel or pot they cannot get out. This method needed none of the constant attention given to 'trunks', therefore more traps could be set and more crabs and lobsters caught.

By 1863 only Flamborough had still not converted to creels and pots and by 1876 'trunking' was no longer used by inshore fishermen at all. Though this new method was successful it had one disadvantage — it could not distinguish the bigger crabs and lobsters from the smaller and younger ones. This was never a problem with 'trunking' as the baby shell fish always fell through the net as the hoop was brought up. As a result, though catches increased for a time, they soon began to diminish due to overfishing so in 1876 Parliament passed an Act stating that no crabs measuring less than four and a half inches across the back should be landed.

Another problem which had made itself evident in the 1850s was the shortage of bait. Cockles and mussels were usually used for this purpose and were normally collected by women and children at the water's edge. However, this humble method could not cope with the growth in demand and so inshore fishermen had to look elsewhere for their bait. What made their task all the more difficult was that cockles and mussels were becoming an increasingly popular delicacy for human consumption and to further the problem, some were being used for manure on farmers' fields. It was not long before cockles and mussels began to be overfished themselves and despite many unsuccessful attempts to introduce restrictions, the price of these shell fish began to rise uncontrollably. In the 1860s the Yorkshire coast inshore fishing reached its peak — a peak which it had never reached before or since.

It was the massive expansion around this period that caused a labour shortage in the fishing industry and from the 1850s, to meet this demand, the boy apprentice was introduced. Apprentices were a cheap, though unreliable, source of labour as they were paid no wages, receiving bed and board for their work. Once bound to the smack-owners, they led a hard life, harshly treated by the other crew members and were severely punished for any wrong-doing or even if another member of the crew simply felt like it. They were often over-worked, especially on the box fleet in which smacks stayed at sea for several weeks at a stretch. Apprentices came from orphanages, workhouses or homes for destitute boys, and once signed up, it proved very difficult for them to leave their new career and one of the only legal alternatives was to buy their way out. However, money was scarce and normally neither the apprentice nor his family could afford this option. There were some cases of suicide, while those who decided to run away were considered to be deserting and if caught were sent to the county gaol.

In 1880 an Act of Parliament was introduced to outlaw the imprisonment of apprentices. At Grimsby absconding was a major problem and a clause from a previous Act of Parliament was used to justify continuing the practice of jailing these impoverished boys. The introduction of steam and government regulation put an end to this gross exploitation and the lot of the apprentices was greatly improved. After the First World War the number of apprentices dramatically dropped with the system finally abolished in the 1930s partly due to the slump in market forces.

The eighteenth century brought mixed fortunes for the fishing industry along the Yorkshire coast. The main harbour ports of the area, Whitby, Scarborough and Bridlington Quay, had all concentrated their resources on other maritime pursuits such as shipbuilding and whaling, causing fishing to suffer as a result. Other ports tended to rely on their small fishing fleets, at the mercy to the fluctuations of the industry.

The vessels used for fishing were usually cobles, flat-bottomed clinker-built fishing craft normally associated with the Yorkshire coast with each port having its own design which would slightly differ from the rest. The other fishing vessel which was widely in use in the northern ports was the versatile three-masted lugger. Known as 'five-man boats', though they usually carried more, they could often be seen around the beginning of each autumn, travelling down the east coast to ports such as Great Yarmouth, where they would join the herring fishing season. On the vessels return home at the start of November, they would be laid up for the winter months until the following spring when they would be equipped to catch white fish once again. The largest lugger fleets among the Yorkshire ports belonged to Staithes and Filey, despite their apparent lack of size and facilities to cope with these large vessels.

Staithes and Filey were the leading Yorkshire 'lining' fisheries, which was still considered the most important form of fishing in the 1830s. 'Liners' or 'codmen' caught fish on long lines of baited hooks and concentrated on catching quality fish. This era saw the industry no longer confined to the local market, exporting their catch to inland Britain,

COGAN'S CHARITY,

FOR

BINDING BOYS APPRENTICE.

◆•◆

WE, the undersigned, ~~do hereby agree to~~ *have*
take~~n~~ *Arthur Anthony Kirkup*

as an Apprentice, for the term of *Seven*
Years. commencing *February 23rd 1914*
to teach him the trade of a *Shipwright*
and to pay him the Wages following :—

FIRST YEAR, per Week .... 4/.

SECOND YEAR   ,, ... 4/.

THIRD YEAR   ,, ... 5/.

FOURTH YEAR   ,, ... 6/.

FIFTH YEAR   ,, ... 7/.

SIXTH YEAR   ,, ... 8/.

SEVENTH YEAR   ,, ... 9/.

For HELLYERS' STEAM FISHING CO. LTD.

Signed *[signature]*
Secy & Director

N.B.—*Any further particulars required to be inserted in the Indenture
must be stated in this Certificate.*

A document recording the apprenticeship of A. A. Kirkup to Hellyers. The Hellyers were originally from Devon and remained involved in Hull's fishing industry until the 1960s. Alderman Cogan, an eighteenth century philanthropist, endowed a charity school and a fund which supported young men and women embarking on employment for the first time.

Photograph showing Grimsby cod fishermen and two young apprentices. The typical crew was three men and two boys who had to handle the rigging, the trawl net, gut the fish or stow it or box it. Until the arrival of the steam winch in the late nineteenth century, all the main jobs were done using muscle power aided by tackles and winches.

By 1872 apprentices in Grimsby outnumbered adult fishermen by 1,350 to 1,150.

London and Spain. When these exports dried up, lining lost its importance to trawling and herring fishing.

Trawling was introduced to the east coast around the 1840s using beam trawls, which is a large net towed along the bottom of the sea with its mouth held open with the aid of a wooden beam. The original trawling vessels were the sailing smacks, which by the 1870s had been developed and enlarged. Among the many alterations was the insertion of a well in the hull so that the fish could be carried and kept fresh.

When the herrings changed their waters from the Baltic to the North Sea around 1427, few people recognised the wealth which came with them. Notably among the few who did, were the Dutch, who dominated the early years of this industry with their larger ships and their method of curing at sea, which remained a secret for over one hundred years. In 1494 their stranglehold grew tighter when a treaty was made allowing them to fish off the coast of England. This angered the home fleets and had a devastating effect on the British fishing industry, as rather than compete with their foreign rivals, the home boats were contented with buying the fish off them instead. Attempts to re-establish the waning industry by Charles I, Oliver Cromwell and Charles II were not altogether successful, though they did manage to stir some enthusiasm amongst British fishermen.

Once the influence of the Dutch on the trade waned, due to the Napoleonic Wars (1803 – 1815) blocking their access to fishing grounds, it was not long before the Scottish fleets took over the leadership of the industry. The Scots would follow the fish as they migrated annually down the east coast, and land their catch at the nearest port. It was this method which was largely responsible for making Great Yarmouth the leading herring port in the world.

At the end of each summer the town would play host to scores of Scottish herring drifters and the now famous packing girls, who came down from their homeland by train. These girls — known as girls or lasses irrespective of age — stayed at local boarding houses which were stripped bare of comforts to provide very basic accommodation. Their job involved gutting and packing the herring with alternate layers of salt into a barrel, ready to export them to the Baltic ports and Germany. The sale of herrings on the Yorkshire coast however was concentrated on the home market. Whitby, Scarborough and Staithes were used as landing ports for the Scottish fleets too, and by 1852 the number of visiting vessels fishing out of Scarborough equalled the town's own number. Before the middle of the nineteenth century, there was slow but steady growth within the industry, but it was the slowness of this expansion which caused concern and was blamed on the reluctance of fishermen to experiment and introduce new fishing methods.

On 9th June 1860 disaster struck Filey's small fishing fleet when thirteen of the town's twenty two strong fleet of yawls were lost during a horrendous gale. However, all loss of property, around £10,000 worth, was reimbursed to the fishermen of Filey over the next three years.

In the 1860s, though most individual catches fluctuated between very good and very bad, the very good catches caused a seasonal increase in the number of herrings caught. In the 1870s the introduction of a steam tug at Scarborough, used to tow the sailing boats to and from the fishing grounds when weather conditions prevented them from

Scottish fisher girls on the South Denes at Great Yarmouth. Their job involved gutting and packing the herring with alternate layers of salt into a barrel, ready to export them to the Baltic ports and Germany. Onlookers were often amazed at the speed and the dexterity of the 'girls', who worked through all weathers with no shelter from the harsh elements. These girls, (known as girls or lassies irrespective of age), stayed at some of the town's boarding houses, which were stripped of comforts to provide only the most basic accommodation.

After the merchants had stopped buying the fishermen's catch at Great Yarmouth, the surplus — here seen on one day in 1954 — went to the herring reduction factory for conversion into meal and oil. No sooner had the factory been built at Yarmouth than the herring stocks diminished and there was no longer a 'glut' of fish.

doing it themselves, attracted even more vessels to the port, giving the town the edge over neighbouring Whitby. The building of the railways in the same decade facilitated distribution and so caused an even greater demand for herring, a demand which was to see further intensification of fishing in the North Sea. The prosperity continued, and the Yorkshire coast herring fleet was rated the second largest in England.

Whaling only began to gather any importance in England after the government offered bounties, though there had been frequent unsuccessful attempts to enter the trade by British whalers, mostly from the northern ports. After bounties were introduced, the whaling industry centred upon Hull for a short time, whilst increasing the prosperity of smaller ports, such as Whitby and Gorleston.

Like herring fishing, whaling had been dominated by the Dutch, who operated from Smeerenberg, (translated 'Blubbertown'). They met little competition from the British whaling fleet, which came mainly from Hull, King's Lynn, Yarmouth and London, and which seems to have spent most of its time on internal squabbling! By the 1830s overfishing and the drop in demand for whale oil, caused the decline of the industry in this country. Though whaling proved profitable for many people, it was a wasteful trade, with only a small proportion of the huge carcase being used. The Greenland whale was preferred by the hunters as it was slow and passive and remained buoyant after its killing. However, the killing was slow and tortuous and the whale was often allowed to suffer before it was finally slain.

On sighting the quarry the main whaler would drop its smaller boats into the water so they were able to come into close proximity to the whale, allowing them to shoot a harpoon attached to a rope into the creature from point-blank range. This was not actually meant to kill the whale but was merely to prevent any escape and stop the whale's 'death flurry'. Lances would then be thrust in between its ribs and forced up and down until eventually the poor whale died. The small boats would then make their way triumphantly back to the main ship where the whale would have its baleen and blubber removed, after which the corpse would be discarded. Regrettably, this practice is still pursued today.

By the end of the eighteenth century Hull had firmly established itself as Britain's leading whaling port. The whales were caught, normally in Arctic waters, by the city's own fleets and then would be taken back to factories in Hull to be processed. Hull's last whaler was an auxiliary steamer, the *Diana*, built in 1840 at Bremen and later converted for whaling. From the late 1860s she was the last recognised whaler in the port until 1869 when, returning from a whaling trip, she was wrecked off Lincolnshire, spelling the end of Hull's whaling industry. The demise of the industry had been apparent for the last three decades when it had gradually been replaced by the flourishing deep sea fishing industry.

As early as 1812 steam-powered vessels had been seen on the Clyde and by 1814 they were on the Humber too. The following decades saw many experiments with steam but it was not until the 1870s that it was used extensively by the British fishing fleets. The trawling fleets were the first to make the change from sail to steam in this country, from the late 1870s through to the latter end of the 1880s. By 1900 Hull had become the first port in England to have replaced all of its white fish sailing fleets with steam-powered vessels. The herring industry was far slower in introducing steam and it wasn't until

A painting showing the whaleship, the *William Lee* in the Arctic. Launched at Hull on 17 January 1831 from Messrs Dikes and Gibsons Shipyard, the *William Lee* was built for Robert Lee and John Tall, merchants.

The vessel is shown in three views and the picture illustrates all the main activities involved in hunting and processing the Greenland Right Whale, so called because it was the 'right one' to hunt. On the left in the midground a whale is being harpooned, whilst a dead 'fish' being towed back towards the ship is dominating the foreground. The main topsail is backed up to maintain the ship's position whilst the whale is alongside and the blubber is being stripped off or flensed in whaling parlance. Long 'slips' of blubber are winched aboard then chopped into small pieces for storage in barrels in the hold. The boiling to extract the oil was carried out back in Hull when the vessel returned to Hull in September–October having set out in March or April of the same year.

This painting was commissioned from John Ward (1798-1849) Hull's outstanding marine artist, by Richard Hill, master of the *William Lee*. He was in command in her first season and again in 1832 when no less than 27 whales were caught.

The drawing is based upon a contemporary model of the Whitby whaleship *Harpooner*. Like almost all of the Arctic whalers she was an ordinary merchant ship adapted for the whaling trade. The hull was 'doubled' with an extra layer of planks and internally fortified with stout timbers. Six or seven whaleboats are hung from the davits or laid on top of the crossbeams at the stern of the vessel. Note the blubber guy, a rope slung between fore and main mast with a group of large blocks for hoisting up the strips of blubber.

the final years of the nineteenth century that steam-powered drifters began to make an impact. Not long after this the herring fleets overcame their suspicion of this new form of power and so began the demise of the sailing drifter.

Bridlington was the first Yorkshire port to take the lead in steam trawling, which was having such a slow introduction at neighbouring ports owing to the stubborn resistance of local fishermen to change. This gave the town, who had no strongly established fishing tradition, the opportunity to become the most important inshore trawling port in the area.

From the 1840s all-year trawling was established, associated with the discovery, around this period, of the Silver Pits. The most popular fishing grounds located in the North Sea were the Dogger Bank and Silver Pits, and they were worked by fleets from most of the notable ports from Whitby to Yarmouth and even as far south as Barking in Essex. Indeed, it was Hewett's Short Blue Fleet, from Barking and later Gorleston, who revolutionised trawling with the introduction of 'box fleeting,' which allowed vessels to stay at sea for periods of up to eight weeks. Hewett's owned a large fleet at Gorleston where by 1875 a total of 400 trawling smacks worked for the port. Gorleston, with Yarmouth, became one of the leading trawling ports in the country though lost its importance with the coming of the steam trawling fleets at Grimsby and Hull and in 1903 Hewett's withdrew their interest from the town.

Further progress in the development of the fishing fleet involved the use of propellers. The first purpose-built screw steam trawler was the *Pioneer* from Scarborough which was soon followed by the *Zodiac* from Grimsby. Screw steam trawlers were capable of longer journeys, many travelling as far as North Norway to reach the White Sea off the coast of Russia.

Steam paddle trawlers were only profitable if worked extensively but with poor weather conditions for around a quarter of the year this did not prove possible. In Yorkshire, paddle trawlers, because of their manoeuvrability, could work the grounds close to the rocks where the smacks dare not go, but by the 1880s these small grounds were showing signs of overfishing after being intensively worked for a number of years. Scarborough, where most of the local industry's vessels came from, felt the full effect of this with their steam fleet drastically reducing in numbers. Now it was the turn of Hull and Grimsby to compete for Scarborough's crown as the leading fishing port on the Yorkshire coast, though both went on to become two of the leading fishing centres in the country.

Despite Scarborough's problems, between 1880 and 1883 the town, along with Whitby, saw an increase in the number of vessels landing at their ports. Though record landings were recorded in 1882, the success of the visiting fleet was causing the local vessels to suffer as a result. In 1884 a disaster befell the herring industry when its foreign market collapsed due to over production. The effect on the Yorkshire fleet was minimal as only a small percentage of its catch was sold to the continent, though was felt more at ports such as Yarmouth, where a large proportion was imported. Prices began to fall and many merchants and shipowners went bankrupt, and though the industry recovered with the revival of the foreign markets by 1893, it did not learn its lesson. The rest of the decade saw a continual glut in the herring market with the fishermen catching more and more fish to try to make some profit but instead causing the prices to drop even further.

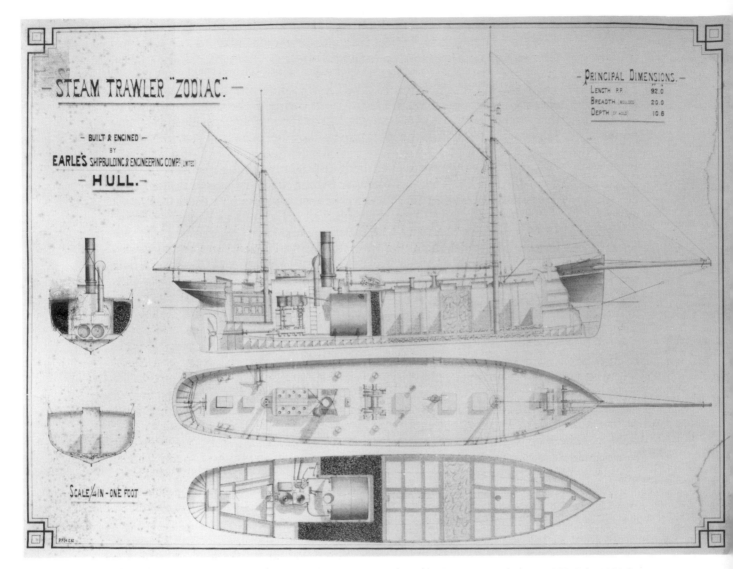

STEAM TRAWLER "ZODIAC."

— BUILT & ENGINED —
BY
EARLE'S SHIPBUILDING & ENGINEERING COMP? LIMITED
— HULL.—

PRINCIPAL DIMENSIONS.
LENGTH P.P.   92.0
BREADTH (MOULDED) 20.0
DEPTH (OF HOLD)   10.6

SCALE 1/4 IN · ONE FOOT

This general arrangement plan depicts the steam trawler *Zodiac* launched by Earles of Hull in 1881 for the Grimsby and North Sea Trawling Co. She and the *Pioneer* of Scarborough were the first purpose built steam trawlers ever to be built. The *Zodiac* was 92 feet long, and as an insurance against engine failure and probably also to economise on fuel, she retained a full suite of sails. In the space of a little more than a decade such vessels had completely replaced the sailing smack in the Hull fleet though the process took rather longer in Grimsby.

With the introduction of steam to fishing around the turn of the century, vessels were able to fish in windless conditions and were able to go further afield and for longer, with steam trawlers able to exploit the grounds off Iceland and Norway and still returning quickly enough for their catch to be edible. However, the ports on the Yorkshire coast had difficulty financing conversion to steam and suffered as a result. The dwindling fortunes of the fishing industry on the Yorkshire coast saw stations such as Staithes and Filey reduced to inshore fishing status while Bridlington Quay, Scarborough and Whitby would never again reach the same heights of the area's fishing heyday around the 1870s. They could simply not keep pace with the development of fishing, which had advanced and now relied on the bigger ports with modern facilities such as Hull and Great Yarmouth. The blame also rests with the relentless and ruthless way in which the North Sea fishing grounds off parts of the Yorkshire coast were overfished and made redundant during the nineteenth century, moving the focus of the fleets away from the area.

Though the Yorkshire coast fishing industry was facing an alarming decline in the early 1900s, Great Yarmouth was entering its most successful phase as a fishing centre. The years leading up to World War One saw the zenith of herring fishing as a whole, with 1913 regarded as the most prosperous year in its history with 835 million herrings landed by 1,163 drifters in Yarmouth alone, many of these belonging to the Scottish fleets, who were a major factor in the boom of the industry. The trawler fleets were also at the height of their prosperity, landing huge catches of cod and plaice from the prolific fishing grounds in the North Sea, with Hull regarded as the world's leading deep-sea fishing centre.

In 1913 the herring industry reached its peak, and like all peaks is followed by a sharp decline. The war interrupted the industry at its height and left fond memories in the minds of fishermen who were serving their country with dreams of the many great harvests of fish to come. Upon their return these dreams had turned into nightmares, as the country they came back to was a country in the grips of depression and hardship. Most of fishing's export industry had gone, as Russia, Poland and Germany could not afford to buy and though the fish stocks had been replenished during the war years, they soon began to show signs of depletion.

During the First World War steam trawlers and drifters had been adapted to perform the role of minesweeping, with many new vessels being built on the orders of the Navy. After the war these vessels were converted to fishing purposes and were offered for sale though it was not long before they were replaced by more modern steam vessels. In the Second World War trawlers were used for a number of different purposes such as escorting convoys, hunting U-boats and minesweeping, but on their return to British shores after the victorious war campaign, the steam trawlers were replaced by diesel-powered vessels. The era of steam was over.

In 1946 the first oil-powered trawlers were introduced and though at first it was believed the catch would taste and smell of oil, this myth was soon proved wrong. The following years saw the advent of the side-fishing trawler. Side-fishing was a hazardous method of fishing with frequent maiming and even death featuring in the industry. The nets were dropped over the side of the vessel though when it was time to winch the trawl up, the method used sometimes unbalanced the trawler and threatened to capsize the vessel. In the 1950s side-trawlers were replaced by the stern trawler, which used a different system of hauling up the trawl from a stern ramp which avoided unbalancing the vessel. The two hundred and eighty foot *Faitry* was the first of these new vessels, but proved to be an unprofitable venture though its successor, *Faitry II*, which actually froze its catch whilst at sea, met with more success. Another type is the factory trawler, which not only freeze their catch at sea but gut and fillet the fish on board too, with the aid of built-in machinery.

The result of the Cod Wars of 1958, 1972 and 1975 was a 200 mile exclusion zone around Iceland for the British fleets. This, coupled with E.E.C. limitations, meant that deep-sea fishing fleets like those from Hull, suddenly had nowhere to ply their trade. 'The higher you are, the further you fall', and Hull's vast fishing industry fell flat and has only now just begun on the slow road to recovery. The possible extent of this recovery is still in the balance, partly owing to the precarious state of fish stocks in the North Sea.

During the Second World War, as in the 1914 War, the stocks of fish had dramatically increased due to the suspension of sea fishing. In 1946 a new era seemed to beckon, with plentiful shoals widespread throughout the depths of the sea. Soon our local fleets were joined by international fleets from the Netherlands and Poland and even the Scottish fleets returned once again to the east coast ports. However, quotas were set by the Ministry of Food which once fulfilled meant that the surplus herring catch had to be used for fertiliser or animal food, and on occasions were even thrown back into the sea. By the mid-1950s a gloom had set over the industry with the stocks of herring becoming exhausted and those fish which were caught becoming smaller. This was blamed on the Russian and Dutch factory ships which fished indiscriminately, netting all the young herring with the mature fish. The final nail in the coffin was the arrival of the 'efficient' German fishing fleet, which left hardly any room for British boats.

In 1975 herring fishing was placed under a ban and though unscrupulous foreign fishermen continued to fish the North Sea off the Danish coast, this too was eventually stopped, though not until nine years later! With the ban on herring fishing being lifted in the 1980s a resurgence of hope was felt, though looking ahead, the future appears precarious for our fishermen. Modern day fishing, with all its restrictions and the arguments regarding insufficient quotas, will continue to prove difficult for all involved. Demand has dropped too, but it must be hoped that the industry can be restored and regain the glories of its past.

Sustaining a living from the hand of nature is a life which, at times, can go unrewarded and is filled with danger in the most trying conditions. Any romantic view of a 'life at sea' can be quickly dispelled as accidents are common and it is estimated that one fishermen dies every eight days. Yet still they continue to work the seas, in an industry which, for most, is in their blood and part of them. A part which will never be lost, long after they have hung up their nets for the last time.

The 'Mission' smack under tow. Note that she is London registered and carrying a full complement of fishing gear. Even early this century the Mission vessels, which were by then modern steamers, were helping to pay their way by actively engaging in fishing. A smack called the *Ensign* was purchased in 1882 by Ebenezer Mather and sailed out of Yarmouth with supplies of Bibles, literature, warm clothing, tobacco and medicine. These efforts culminated in the formation of the Royal National Mission to Deep Sea Fishermen in 1884, whose work continues to this day giving help both physically and spiritually to shipwrecked, sick or disabled fishermen, their wives, widows and children.

In the days of the sailing trawler, when the society was founded, the casualty rate was high and the North Sea was plagued by the 'coopers' selling cheap liquor.

Page 103

The cod end being winched up the ramp of the *Junella*. As soon as it was on deck the cod end knot would be released and the catch dropped below decks where it would be washed and then deep frozen. The advent of stern-fishing also meant the arrival of refrigeration at sea. Previously fish had only been chilled by packing in layers of crushed ice. The old method meant that the maximum duration of a voyage was about three weeks after which the fish rapidly deteriorated.

Page 104

Trawling by towing the net over the side of the vessel can be traced back to the Middle Ages. The early trawls were fitted with a beam which kept the mouth of the net open allowing the fish to enter. Towards the end of the nineteenth century this was replaced by the otter trawl in which two otter boards or trawl doors were attached to the towing wires to achieve the same effect. The elimination of the beam meant that the trawl nets could be made bigger, giving the steam trawlers greater catching power. The optimum length of the beam was fifty feet.

The next great revolution in fishing techniques had to wait until 1961 when Hull acquired its first stern fishing vessel the *Lord Nelson* quickly followed by J. Marr's *Junella*. Here the bulging cod end can be seen on the deck of the *Junella* — note the large slip knot at the end.

Page 105

Aboard a Hull side-fishing trawler, colloquially a 'side-winder' in the 1960s. The mate, arms akimbo, has just released the cod end knot and the fish tumble out on the deck. After gutting they were sorted and washed, tasks all done on the deck exposed to the elements. When on a good ground the men were kept busy shooting and hauling the nets and would sometimes work for maybe 17 hours at a stretch, often in sub-arctic conditions. Another advantage of the stern trawlers which replaced the 'side-winder' was that the processing was done below the decks under cover.

Page 106

This photograph illustrates fish being 'shelved'. The fish are laid head to tail and surrounded by crushed ice. Each layer is then divided horizontally by fish-boards, made of wood or (more recently) of aluminium, thus lessening the possibility of damage by bruising and crushing.

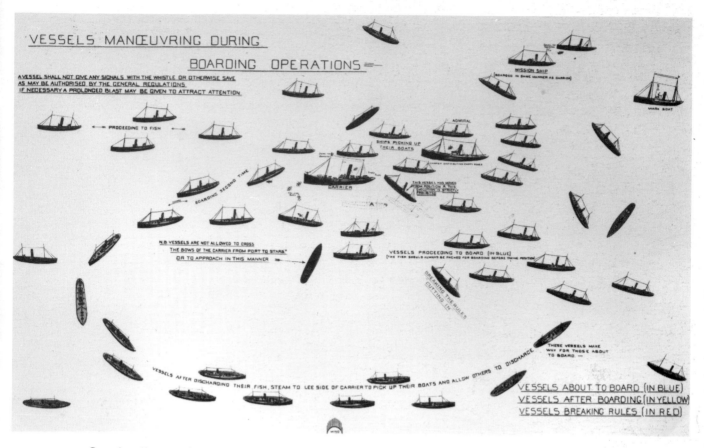

Complex diagram showing the regulations which had to be followed by the boxing fleet.

The box system was established in Hull by John Sims, surviving until 1936 when due to falling catches and the rising cost of coal, the Gamecock fleet went into receivership. By then the 'single-boaters', fishing independently off Iceland and Norway, dominated the Hull fishing scene and efficient railway connections from Hull meant that fish packed in crushed ice could be rushed to London or any of the big cities whilst still in top condition. Much of it was bought by the multitude of fish shops which provided a large selection of the population in the industrial centres with wholesome meals.

The largest of the box fleets was that of the Kelsall Bros. and Beeching, who became known as the 'Gamecock fleet' owing to the symbol of a red cockerel on a white flag painted on the funnel. They restricted their activities to the North Sea and the fish was transferred daily to a fast steam cutter mostly for delivery to Billingsgate in London. This Gamecock trawler flies the flag of the 'Admiral' or 'Don' skipper, whose job it was to control the movements of the vessels under his command.

After emptying the trawl net onto the deck, the fish was packed in boxes (hence the box fleet), passed over the side and piled into a rowing boat for transfer to the cutter. The dangers of loading and unloading in anything more than the gentlest of swells is obvious and there were numerous casualties.

The Admiral's ship of the 'Gamecock fleet'.

Preparing fish for curing at Grimsby in the 1930s, showing the fish being split and salted.

The fish were then dried, seen here at the West Marsh, Grimsby. Because of the climate, curing could only be done in the summer months, reaching its peak from July to September.

The last part of the process was to pack the fish into parcels, for distribution to the merchants.

Two old coble fishermen. The one in the boat is baiting the hooks of a long line. Cobles are still numerous at Bridlington and Flamborough, though are now installed with engines rather than sails.

Crab and lobster pots are still set between February and September, whilst lining is a winter fishery, mainly for cod and haddock. The lines would total twelve in a set, each line having 250 hooks, 3000 in total, extending for up to 3,600 fathoms. Whelks, mussels and limpets are the regular bait.

Selected Bibliography

BEADLE, Barry: *Fifty Miles from Spurn to Goole*

EKBERG, Charles: *Grimsby Fish*
(Barracuda Books, 1984)

FAIRHALL, David: *East Anglian Shores*
(A. C. Black London, 1988)

GARDINER: *History of Wisbech and the Neighbourhood 1848 – 1898*
(1898)

GOODWIN, E. A.: *Cromer Past*

GOOLE LIBRARY: *150 Years of the Port of Goole 1826 – 1976*
(Goole Port Handbooks, 1976)

GOWER, E.: *Scarborough – A Practical Guide for Visitors*
(Dalesman White Rose Guide, 1975)

HEDGES, A. A. C.: *East Coast Shipping*
(Shire Publications, 1974)

OLDHAM, A. A.: *The History of Wisbech River*
(Arthur Artis Oldham, 1933)

PEARSON, Gordon: *Hull and East Coast Fishing*
(City of Kingston upon Hull Museum and Art Galleries, 1976)

PURCHAS, Arthur W.: *Wells-next-the-Sea*
(East Anglian Magazine Ltd, 1965)

ROBINSON, Robb: *A History of the Yorkshire Coast Fishing Industry 1780 – 1914*
(Hull University Press, 1987)

SAVIN, Alfred Collinson: *Savin's History of Cromer*
(Rance & Worthy, 1937)

TEMPLE, C. R.: *Clifford Temple Remembers Norwich*
(Panda Books Publishing, 1983)

TEMPLE, C. R.: *Clifford Temple Remembers Great Yarmouth and Gorleston*
(Panda Books Publishing, 1984)

THOMPSON: *Hull's Side-Fishing Trawling Fleet 1946 – 86*
(Hutton Press, 1986)

WALCOTT, M. E. C.: *East Coast of England*
(Edward Stanford, 1861)

WREN, W.: *East Coast Ports*
(Terence Dalton, 1973)